NEW VANGUARD 349

WARSHIPS AT DUNKIRK 1940

ANGUS KONSTAM ILLUSTRATED BY EDOUARD A. GROULT

OSPREY PUBLISHING
Bloomsbury Publishing Plc
Kemp House, Chawley Park, Cumnor Hill, Oxford OX2 9PH, UK
Bloomsbury Publishing Ireland Limited,
29 Earlsfort Terrace, Dublin 2, D02 AY28, Ireland
1359 Broadway, 12th Floor, New York, NY 10018, USA
E-mail: info@ospreypublishing.com
www.ospreypublishing.com

OSPREY is a trademark of Osprey Publishing Ltd

First published in Great Britain in 2026

A catalogue record for this book is available from the British Library.

ISBN: PB 9781472872555; eBook 9781472872562; ePDF 9781472872579; XML 9781472872548

26 27 28 29 30 10 9 8 7 6 5 4 3 2 1

Index by Mark Swift
Typeset by Lumina Datamatics Ltd
Printed by Repro India Ltd.

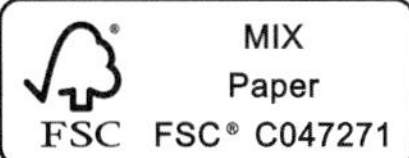

Title page caption:
'Withdrawal from Dunkirk, June 1940', a painting by the Admiralty war artist, Richard Ernst Eurich (1903–1992), was used as the Royal Navy's official Christmas Card in December 1940. Although Eurich wasn't at Dunkirk, it was based on first-hand accounts and testimonies. This is a copy, from the archives of the late David Lyon – the original is in the collection of the National Maritime Museum, Royal Museums, Greenwich.

All photos from 'The Stratford Archive'.

CONTENTS

WARSHIPS AT DUNKIRK 1940

INTRODUCTION

Almost as soon as the last exhausted troops made it safely home, the evacuation of the British Expeditionary Force from Dunkirk has been lauded as a 'miracle'. Even at the time, cheering crowds lined the streets to welcome the 'Tommies' home, and somehow, in the British psyche, a humiliating defeat was turned into something of a victory – 'one in the eye for Herr Hitler', as one British newspaper declared. Other rose-tinted myths have grown up around it too. One is that Britain was saved in its darkest hour by the 'Little Ships of Dunkirk', manned by amateur sailors and fishermen, who snatched an army of plucky British soldiers from the beaches of Dunkirk, and spirited home, from under the very noses of the all-conquering Germans.

In Britain, the term 'Dunkirk spirit' is still seen as a show of sangfroid or grit in the face of adversity, and a cheerful and patriotic collective refusal to accept defeat. The term, though, like the rescue by the 'Little Ships', isn't based completely on myth, but it ignores an awful lot of reality to shoehorn the myth into place. At its most basic level – the turning of a defeat into a victory – there is no real doubt that, for the Allies, the Dunkirk campaign was a disaster. Dunkirk was a major defeat, as the British and French commanders were outmanoeuvred and outfoxed by their German opponents, and so their troops, however courageous they might have been, were outfought.

In one of the iconic images of the Dunkirk evacuation, the naval trawler HMT *Topaze* is shown laden with French troops, while towing the motorboat of a British destroyer. Usually, these trawlers were used to lift troops from the beach, before transferring them to larger vessels, waiting in the Dunkirk Roads.

The Royal Navy has a historic tradition of 'having the army's back' and rescuing British troops from impending disaster, as achieved at Corunna and Gallipoli. At Dunkirk though, the Navy paid a heavy price for this, losing six destroyers and 24 smaller warships and auxiliaries, with over 40 more vessels damaged. However, this evacuation was achieved because, in 1940, the Royal Navy 'controlled the sea' in

At the same time as 'Withdrawal from Dunkirk, June 1940', Richard Eurich painted a companion piece, 'Dunkirk Beaches, May 1940', focusing on the evacuation from the beaches. This is a copy, from the archives of the late David Lyon – the original is in the collection of the National Gallery of Canada in Ottawa.

naval parlance, and had both the numeric strength and the professional skill to ensure the evacuation was a strategic success. As a result, the British Army had a core around which it could rebuild, forging a new expanded army which could then take the fight to the enemy. The French troops too, for the most part, became the nucleus of a Free French corps, which four years later would liberate Paris.

While not denigrating the efforts of the 'Little Ships', post-war analysis of the Dunkirk evacuation showed that of the 338,682 Allied troops saved at Dunkirk, over 80 per cent of them were lifted to safety aboard Royal Navy warships or naval auxiliary vessels, and another 10 per cent by their French naval counterparts. This book aims to underline this impressive achievement, by placing its emphasis not on the myths of Dunkirk, but on the warships and crews who sailed over to Dunkirk and got the job done.

BACKGROUND

On 20 May 1940, just ten days after their invasion of France began, German troops reached the English Channel near Abbeville, splitting the Allied armies in two. The following day, Lord Gort, commander of the British Expeditionary Force (BEF), ordered a general retreat to the coast. Fortunately, at that key moment, Hitler's controversial 'Halt Order' paused the German offensive, buying time for the Allied withdrawal towards Dunkirk, where the troops hoped they could be evacuated.

Fortunately for Lord Gort, the plans for this evacuation had already been created, and the ships gathered to help carry it out. A week before the evacuation got underway, on 19 May, the British Admiralty appointed V. Adm. Bertram Ramsay to plan this evacuation, which was codenamed Operation *Dynamo*. The 57-year-old Ramsay, a veteran of World

Here, British troops aboard a personnel ship – the small naval-manned Dutch-coaster HMS *Aegir* (Lt. William Whitworth) – watch as French troops aboard a French naval trawler prepare to leave Dunkirk harbour on 28 May.

V. Adm. Bertram Ramsay (1883–1945), the Commander-in-Chief, Dover, was the architect of Operation *Dynamo*. From his headquarters beneath Dover Castle, Ramsay and his small staff organized the Dunkirk evacuation, and achieved what had at first seemed impossible. If there was a 'Miracle of Dunkirk', it was one created by Ramsay.

War I, had retired two years before, but in 1939 he was recalled into service, promoted, and made the Flag Officer in Charge, Dover.

During the 'Phoney War', the 'Dover Command' had been a backwater, and Ramsay, ensconced in his underground headquarters carved out of the rock below Dover Castle, busied himself organizing coastal convoys. With the help of a singularly gifted deputy, Cdr. Frederic 'Johnny' Walker, the future U-boat hunter, he also saw to the blocking of the Dover Straits to enemy U-boats. It made sense that Ramsay, the Royal Navy's 'man on the spot', was given the task of discreetly planning for the worst – the possible evacuation of the BEF and its French Allies from the French coast. His new job then was to save an army.

Operation *Dynamo*

The evacuation of an army from a hostile shore wasn't a new challenge for the Royal Navy. It had performed the task in previous wars and saw 'having the army's back' as part of its remit. During the last war, it had done it at Gallipoli, while throughout the Dunkirk evacuation the Navy was also evacuating Allied forces from Norway. What made Operation *Dynamo* different was the sheer number of beleaguered Allied troops. So, on 19 May, when Ramsay was presented with the task, he was under no illusion that the evacuation could well be both a risky and costly venture.

Ramsay had had his own Dover Command at hand and other warships were being sent to reinforce it. Many of these warships were World War I era destroyers or minesweepers, while others were auxiliary warships: merchant vessels pressed into service. These included former cross-channel ferries and packets, coasters and trawlers. The French Navy also provided its *Pas de Calais* (Strait of Dover) Flotilla, based at Dunkirk, and some Belgian tugs were available. In all, once assembled, Ramsay would have over 150 Allied

The French destroyer *L'Adroit*, which entered service in 1929, was beached after being damaged in a German air attack just off Dunkirk on 21 May. *L'Adroit* remained there throughout the subsequent evacuation, when the stricken ship was bombed again, and her bow was blown off. Here, German troops are seen visiting the wreck at low tide.

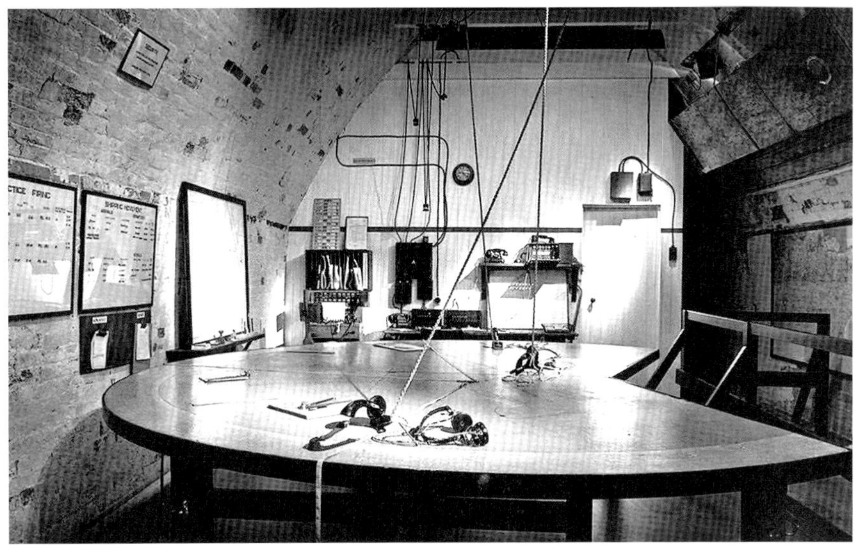

V. Adm. Ramsay and his staff, including the future U-boat hunter Capt. Walker, controlled the naval side of the evacuation from this underground Operations Room beneath Dover Castle. This reconstruction of the Ops Room forms the centrepiece of the underground complex, which is maintained by English Heritage.

warships of various types at his disposal, ranging from a cruiser to small motor launches. Augmenting them were hundreds of smaller requisitioned vessels, the fishing boats and pleasure craft which became the 'Little Ships of Dunkirk'. Assembling the vessels was the easy part. Using them to evacuate an army under fire was the real challenge.

A fast-moving situation

The evacuation of a third of a million men was always going to be a tough proposition. The evacuation had to be set in motion within days, yet Ramsay still didn't have all the ships he'd need. Planning had to be improvised, and Ramsay's 16-strong staff housed in casemates beneath Dover Castle would have to overcome a string of challenges to make *Dynamo* happen. What made it tougher was that this evacuation would have to be carried out in the face of heavy air attacks, and possibly interference from the other German services. Few would have blamed Ramsay if these challenges couldn't be overcome. Meanwhile the situation on the ground was changing rapidly, and there was every chance that the encircled Allied troops would be forced to surrender before the Royal Navy could come to their aid. The following day, Prime Minister Churchill told the Admiralty that he thought 30,000 British troops might be saved. Ramsay was more optimistic, thinking about 45,000 troops could be brought off. The fact that the final number was ten times more than Churchill's estimate was the true 'miracle' of Dunkirk.

Ramsay's initial plan was to utilize the ports of Boulogne, Calais and Dunkirk. On 22 May, though, the Germans advanced on both Boulogne and Calais, which ruled out their use for *Dynamo*. Meanwhile, German Army Group B was pressing the Allies along a line stretching from the Schelde to the French border near Mons. That put them within 40 miles of Dunkirk. The French General Blanchard,

As the Senior Naval Officer (SNO) Dunkirk, Capt. William Tennant was Ramsay's 'man on the ground' in Dunkirk, assisted by a naval party of 168 officers and men. He and his men supervised the evacuation of the Allied troops from the port, the beaches and the East Mole. Tennant remained at his post until the evacuation was completed on 2 June.

whose army was concentrated around Lille, had 'no thought of retreat', while Lord Gort's BEF near Courtai (Kortrijk) also planned to hold the line. However, that day, fresh orders told him his priority was the preservation of the BEF. So, he should plan for a withdrawal towards the coast, just in case. Lord Gort began the move the following day.

Arguably, what bought Ramsay the time he needed was Hitler's controversial 'Halt Order' of 23 May. Concerned about tank losses, and assured by FM Göring that his Luftwaffe could destroy the Allied pocket, Hitler ordered Gen. Rundstedt's Army Group A to hold its positions. On the coast at Gravelines, Gen. Guderian's XIX Panzer Corps was just 10 miles west of Dunkirk, and about to launch an assault which, without doubt, would have captured the port. The Halt Order put paid to that and offered Ramsay a ray of hope. The fighting would continue in the east, where FM von Bock's Army Group B received no such order. By the end of that day, though, after Gort's contraction of his line, the pocket formed a triangle based on the coast between Gravelines and Zeebrugge, with its apex around Lille. The French held the line from Gravelines to Lille, the eastern side of the triangle was held by the British as far as Ypres, while the Belgians extended the line to the coast near Ostend. Boulogne and Calais, however, were irretrievably cut off.

Boulogne and Calais

In Boulogne, the perimeter was manned by British and French troops, aided by several British destroyers, which performed naval gunfire support (NGS) bombardments in support of the defenders. That afternoon they were joined by nine French destroyers of the *Pas de Calais* Flotilla, amid heavy air attacks which claimed the French destroyer *Orage*, while others

A

THE BRITISH DESTROYERS HMS *KEITH* AND HMS *WORCESTER*

1. HMS *Keith* (D06). HMS *Keith* was a 'flotilla leader', her design incorporating the extra accommodation and communications equipment needed by the 'Captain (D)', the officer commanding a destroyer flotilla. In May 1940, *Keith* served as the flotilla leader for Capt. David Simson, commander of the 19th DF (Destroyer Flotilla), attached to the Dover Command. When Simson was killed off Boulogne on 23 May, Capt. Edward Berthon assumed command of both *Keith* and the flotilla. On the night of 30–31 May, *Keith* evacuated 992 soldiers from Dunkirk. The following night, *Keith* returned, this time as the flagship of R. Adm. Frederic Wake-Walker, who was supervising these night operations. The following morning, while the destroyer was still lying off the beach near La Panne, *Keith* was dive-bombed, and a near-miss damaged the ship's steering gear. While this was being repaired, the ship was caught in a second attack, and a bomb dropped into the aft funnel, wrecking the boiler room and starting a major fire. Berthon gave the order to abandon ship, and *Keith* sank there at 0945hrs. In all, 36 of her crew were killed. Here, *Keith* is shown as the ship appeared during Operation *Dynamo*.

2. HMS *Worcester* (D96). HMS *Worcester* was typical of the World War I-era Royal Navy destroyer. When built, these V & W class destroyers were some of the most powerful warships of their kind, but two decades later they were largely relegated to convoy escort duties. *Worcester* had been 'in mothballs' before the war, but the destroyer was re-commissioned and sent to fight. *Worcester* was serving with the 16th DF, based in Portsmouth, but on 27 May the destroyer was sent to reinforce the Dover Command for Operation *Dynamo*. In all, *Worcester*, commanded by Cdr. John Allison, made six trips to Dunkirk between 28 May and 1 June, rescuing 4,661 soldiers – the highest total of any of Dover Command's destroyers. On 1 June though, *Worcester* came under repeated Stuka attack in Dunkirk Roads, and although never hit directly, the destroyer was riddled by splinters from almost a hundred near misses. In all, 46 crew and soldiers were killed in the attack, and 180 wounded. Somehow, *Worcester* survived and was towed back to Dover, where the troops were disembarked. This shows *Worcester* as the ship appeared during Operation *Dynamo*.

1

2

The old Modified W-class destroyer HMS *Venomous* (D75), evacuating French women and children from Boulogne, on 23 May. Later, the destroyer began evacuating the men of the Guards Brigade, in the face of heavy air attacks. On the way out of the port, *Venomous* and other accompanying destroyers engaged German tanks and troops, which were pressing the beleaguered Allied defenders.

were damaged. On the evening of 23 May, permission was given to withdraw the troops, and the first were embarked in HMS *Vimiera* and HMS *Whitshed*, which headed for Dover, pursued by dive bombers. The NGS bombardment continued the following day and HMS *Venomous* scored a direct hit on a German tank. During the day, though, the situation ashore became precarious. So, that night, *Vimiera* and HMS *Windsor* rescued what troops they could under cover of darkness. By dawn on 24 May, the Germans had cut off the remainder of the garrison, and so further evacuation was impossible. At 1300hrs the next day, Boulogne fell. Although 5,000 Allied troops were captured, 4,300 more had been evacuated.

Meanwhile, a similar battle was raging in Calais. The Germans launched their assault on 24 May. Again, Ramsay's destroyers were on hand to provide NGS missions, and to evacuate the wounded, despite heavy air attacks, which claimed the destroyer HMS *Wessex*. No evacuation orders were issued, though, despite Ramsay's assembly of an evacuation flotilla of trawlers and drifters. However, early on 26 May, the garrison surrendered before they could be sent in. In all, nearly 20,000 Allied soldiers were captured in Calais, including 3,500 British troops. By then, 23 miles to the east at Dunkirk, Operation *Dynamo* was about to begin.

The evacuation plan

The evacuation plan approved by Ramsay involved shuttling ships between Dover and Dunkirk along a pre-planned course, bypassing coastal shoals and minefields. This later became known as Route Z. It ran south-east from Dover to the French coast near Calais, before running east into Dunkirk Roads. In all it was 39 nautical miles long. By 28 May though, it was clear this was too dangerous, as ships were coming under fire from newly captured shore batteries. So, it was deemed only practicable at night, and an alternative route was used instead. This became Route Y, which ran from Dover up the Kent coast past the Goodwin Sands, before running east towards Nieuwpoort. Some 12 miles from the coast it turned to the south-west to Dunkirk. At 89 miles, this was a much longer route, and so its use would slow the pace of the evacuation.

After Belgium's surrender on 28 May, ships were placed at risk of fire from coastal batteries around Nieuwpoort. So, a third, more direct route was created, 55 miles long, running south-east from Dover to within 9 miles of the coast, when it turned south towards Dunkirk. This became Route X. However, it had to be cleared of mines and buoyed before it could be used.

At this stage, Dunkirk's limited port facilities were still fully operational. The harbour itself was small, with its ferry facilities in the centre, linked to the port's railway. Various smaller quays lay on either side. The whole harbour was encompassed by a pair of moles, dubbed East Mole and West Mole by the British, which Ramsay hoped might eventually be used too. If possible, Ramsay hoped to embark troops directly off the beach, using small boats, which could then ferry the men out to larger ships waiting in the Roads. This would be a suitable task for the 'Little Ships'; augmented by warships' seaboats (cutters and whalers), these were gathered and sent over to Dunkirk. To assist manoeuvring inside the harbour, Ramsay deployed his tugs there, to nudge ships into position. If all went well, Ramsay planned for a four-hour turnaround between Dover and Dunkirk. How this would work in practice remained to be seen.

At first, both the British and the French used the port of Dunkirk itself to evacuate troops directly from the port's numerous quaysides. However, the port had a narrow entrance, just 290yds (266m) wide, and when under air attack there was nowhere for the warships to go. So, while the French continued to concentrate on the port, the British preferred to evacuate troops from the East Mole, which allowed greater freedom of movement for the ships.

In practice, Operation *Dynamo* closely followed the plan developed by Ramsay. Between 26 May and 4 June, approximately 330,000 Allied troops were evacuated from Dunkirk and the neighbouring beaches. Of these, three-quarters of these troops reached safety aboard Allied warships, or naval vessels manned by the British or French navies. During this time, the pace of the evacuation depended largely on the state of the tides, as well as the ebb and flow of troop concentrations in the assembly areas.

German opposition mainly came in the form of intensive air attacks, but the use of mines, coastal batteries and attacks by torpedo-armed E-boats and U-boats also played their part. After 1 June, the ferocity of these air attacks led Ramsay to limit the evacuation to the hours of darkness. This book's scope precludes following Operation *Dynamo* in detail. Instead it summarizes its course over these eventful ten days, highlighting the part played by Allied warships in this great undertaking.

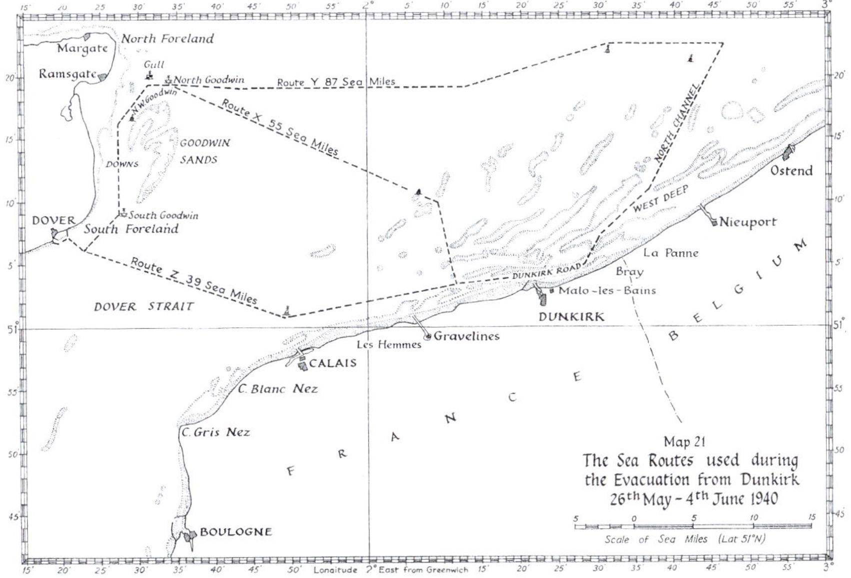

The three evacuation routes used during Operation *Dynamo*. Of these, Route Z was exposed to fire from newly captured coastal batteries near Calais, while a few days later Route Y faced a similar problem, from gun batteries near Nieuwpoort. So, Ramsay ordered Route X to be cleared through the French coastal minefields, which offered a safer passage between Dunkirk and Dover.

Under Lt. Cdr. Arthur Black (centre), the destroyer HMS *Verity* was involved in the evacuation of Allied troops from Boulogne before Operation *Dynamo* began. At 0520hrs on 27 May, as *Verity* was approaching Dunkirk along Route X, the ship came under fire from captured coastal batteries near Calais, and Black, on the destroyer's compass platform, was severely wounded. Sub. Lt. Alington (on the left of the photograph) was also wounded. The First Lieutenant, Lt. Cdr. Eric Jones, duly assumed command. Later that day, Black and the other wounded were landed in Dover. After that, V. Adm. Ramsay decided to avoid Route X, unless under cover of darkness.

Sunday 26 May–Monday 27 May

At 1857hrs on Sunday 26 May, the Admiralty ordered Ramsay to commence Operation *Dynamo*. Ramsay had been prepared, and several 'personnel ships' were already lying in Dunkirk Roads. Unfortunately, only a few of the small craft available were of shallow enough draught to pick up troops from the beach. So, that evening all the troops embarked from Dunkirk harbour. The evacuation went smoothly, and the 'passenger ships' returned, protected by destroyers. The first ship back was SS *Mona's Queen*, a former Manx packet, which arrived in Dover at 2230hrs, and disembarked the first 1,312 BEF troops to make it home. By midnight, the total had climbed to 3,748 men.

The operation was repeated on Monday. Once more the emphasis was on the use of personnel ships, with the destroyers used as cross-channel escorts. They arrived off Dunkirk before dawn (0446hrs), and again priority was given to the wounded. In addition, three personnel ships hadn't left Dunkirk the previous evening, and so made the run home at dawn. In the attempt, HMS *Mona's Isle*, another former Manx packet, was hit by coastal artillery off Gravelines, as was another Manx ship, HMS *King Orry*. Despite this, both ships eventually reached Dover, where they disembarked over 2,500 troops. Later that morning, another personnel ship, the MV *Sequacity*, was sunk by these German guns. As a result, Ramsay decided to abandon the direct route and, at 1100hrs, sent the next batch of evacuation ships to Dunkirk by the longer eastern route (Route Y). Minesweepers were also sent to begin opening a third, more central route (Route X).

That afternoon, Capt. Tennant, the Senior Naval Officer (SNO) Dunkirk, arrived to oversee the evacuation. Due to bombing he declared that the port

The 2,756-ton Isle of Man packet ship SS *Mona's Queen* was requisitioned in September 1939, and was subsequently used as a troopship. The ship took part in the first evacuation of BEF troops on 26–27 May. However, at 0530hrs on 29 May, on returning to Dunkirk, *Mona's Queen* struck a mine off the harbour entrance and sank in less than two minutes. This photograph, taken from the harbour entrance captured that moment when 24 of her crew were killed. Most of them were from the Isle of Man.

was temporarily unusable, and requested small boats be sent to evacuate troops directly from the beaches. By evening, this was being done, with Dutch *shuyts* ('skoots') and drifters ferrying troops out to waiting ships. By midnight, 7,669 troops had been landed in Britain.

The vintage S-class destroyer HMS *Sabre* (H18) of the 22nd DF played a prominent part in Operation *Dynamo*, making a total of ten trips to Dunkirk, between 28 May and 4 June, rescuing a record total of 5,765 Allied troops. Here, the destroyer passes the West Mole at Dunkirk, during an approach to the harbour along Route Z, on the afternoon of 30 May. In the background, the port is ablaze, following a heavy Luftwaffe bombing raid.

Tuesday 28 May–Wednesday 29 May

By Tuesday, the situation ashore had become more perilous, following the Belgian surrender, and heavy German attacks on the pocket. Losses mounted, and a stream of wounded were sent back to Dunkirk. During the day, the Germans occupied Nieuwpoort, meaning they now held coastal batteries overlooking Route Y. The good news for Ramsay was that, after ordering the former cross-channel ferry MV *Queen of the Channel* alongside the East Mole, Tennant was convinced that troops could now embark from it using improvised gangplanks.

So, on Tuesday the embarkation continued, although losses mounted. The first came just after dawn, when the *Queen of the Channel* was bombed and sunk to the east of Dunkirk, on Route Y. That day, most of the evacuation took place from the harbour or the East Mole. The destroyers *Anthony*, *Mackay*, *Montrose*, *Sabre*, *Vimy* and *Worcester* lifted men from the harbour, while other destroyers lay off the beaches, as more troops were ferried out to them.

HMS *Windsor* was attacked and damaged by aircraft while patrolling Route Y, but reached Dover, where hasty repairs were made. Over the course of the day, though, the minesweeper HMS *Brighton Belle* was sunk in a collision with

Relieved British troops entering Dover on the morning of 31 May aboard the World War I vintage destroyer HMS *Venomous* (D75). After disembarking these 1,200 troops, the destroyer made a second run that day, despite being subjected to heavy air attack off the port that evening. In all, *Venomous* made five trips, rescuing a total of 4,410 Allied troops.

British and French troops assembled on the beach to the east of Dunkirk, and in the adjacent dunes, awaiting evacuation under cover of darkness, 28 May. Although there were some instances of panic and indiscipline, for the most part, the majority of these troops waited patiently for their rescue, either by small boats from the beach, or else aboard larger ones, evacuating troops directly from the East Mole.

an unmarked wreck off the Downs, while two naval trawlers and two naval drifters were sunk in air attacks. Despite this, it was a successful day, with 18,527 troops rescued, over 11,000 of them by British destroyers. However, at 0036hrs on Wednesday, halfway along Route Y, the destroyer HMS *Wakeful* was hit by a torpedo fired from the German *Schnellboote* (fast torpedo boat, aka E-boat) S30, and sank with the loss of 740 soldiers and sailors. Then, just at 0350hrs, another destroyer, HMS *Grafton*, was torpedoed nearby, this time by a U-boat, U-62. The crippled destroyer was scuttled later that morning.

A report from Capt. Tennant noted it was impossible to coordinate evacuations with the irregular flow of troops into Dunkirk. On Thursday morning, some 50,000 British troops were awaiting evacuation – men that Tennant's staff described as 'the odds and ends of an army'. The French evacuation had still not officially begun, save for the wounded, but that morning French destroyers and auxiliaries evacuated 3,000 non-essential troops, and wounded. The British evacuation also picked up pace, thanks to the arrival of reinforcements, including destroyers and 'skoots'. Unfortunately for the Allies, although low cloud delayed the arrival of the Luftwaffe, by Thursday afternoon Dunkirk came under heavy air attack. The Royal Air Force (RAF) did what it could, deploying large air groups over the port, but their loitering time there was limited, and the Luftwaffe was able to launch five large-scale attacks between these RAF patrols. Allied losses were heavy. The auxiliary AA ship HMS *Crested Eagle*, a paddle-wheeler, was bombed and beached off Dunkirk, as was another paddle-wheeler, the auxiliary minesweeper HMS *Waverley*, together with two naval trawlers and a drifter.

Of these attacks, the third one, at 1750hrs, was the most devastating. The modern destroyer HMS *Grenade* was hit by two bombs while lying alongside the inner edge of the East Mole. With the destroyer ablaze and sinking, it drifted into the harbour, where it exploded and sank at 2000hrs. Eighteen crewmen were killed in the attack. The bombs also narrowly missed the destroyer HMS *Verity*, which cast off from the Mole during the attack, and made it safely into Dover with 315 troops aboard.

Half an hour before sunset, at 1830hrs, the Stukas returned and caught HMS *Crested Eagle* pulling away from the seaward side of the mole. The old paddle-wheeler was hit by four bombs and set ablaze, and so it was beached. Some 200 of the 600 troops on board survived the attack, but many were badly burned. The survivors were eventually transferred to the destroyer HMS *Sabre* and a trio of minesweepers, and so finally reached Dover. The French had suffered losses too. The third attack at 1750hrs had caught three of their destroyers in the harbour. *Mistral* was badly damaged, but all three made it out of the port, manoeuvring past three Belgian tugs which had also been sunk in the attack.

It had been a traumatic day for the Allies, and a costly one. Still, it was also the most successful evacuation yet, with 50,331 troops landed safely in Britain, including 655 Frenchmen. Ramsay understood the Dunkirk pocket

The paddlewheel minesweeper HMS *Waverley* (J51), commanded by Lt. Cdr. John Cameron RNVR, was built on the Clyde in 1899, and served as an excursion vessel in the Clyde estuary, before being requisitioned and converted into an auxiliary minesweeper, forming part of the 12th M/S Flotilla. In the evening of 28 May, while returning from Dunkirk with 600 troops embarked, *Waverley* was attacked by a dozen He 111s. Two bombers were shot down, but the paddle-wheeler was sunk, and over 100 soldiers and crew lost their lives.

was under heavy pressure from the Germans, and that the defences could cave in with little warning. So, he was keen to maintain the pace of the evacuation over the coming days. Despite the mounting losses, Ramsay had reason to be optimistic. There was a growing number of small boats arriving, which allowed the beach evacuation to be stepped up. However, he decided not to use personnel ships during daylight again, as they were too vulnerable to air attack. That meant destroyers would have to take their place.

B

AIR ATTACK ON THE EAST MOLE, 1745HRS, WEDNESDAY 29 MAY 1940

On Wednesday afternoon, the fourth day of the evacuation, the embarkation of troops from the East Mole went well, despite two enemy air attacks at 1530hrs and 1630hrs. Neither achieved much, and the operation continued, with warships and personnel ships leaving safely, and returning to Britain, their decks crammed with exhausted but grateful troops. Sunset that day was at 2054hrs, and the SNO Dunkirk, Capt. William Tennant RN, began to hope his luck would hold until then. The tide was falling, though, making it slightly harder and slower to embark troops, while the flow of men awaiting evacuation was intermittent.

However, at 1730hrs Tennant's hopes were dashed. The Luftwaffe returned, and this time their attack was pressed home with a ferocious determination. At the time, lying alongside the outer (or eastern) side of the mole was the troopship SS *Fenella* and HMS *Crested Eagle*, a civilian paddle-wheeler, converted into an auxiliary anti-aircraft ship. On the inner (or western) side was the modern destroyer HMS *Grenade*, six naval trawlers lying three abreast, and the older destroyer HMS *Verity*.

The German Ju 87 'Stukas' attacked in waves, a few minutes apart. In this second one, at 1745hrs, *Grenade* took two direct hits, one bomb plunging through the destroyer's foredeck, killing 18 men and igniting a raging fire below decks. Across the mole, *Fenella* suffered a near-miss, which damaged her propellers. A few minutes later, the former Isle of Man packet would be hit by three more bombs, and sunk, while further ahead *Crested Eagle* was also struck by a bomb, and set ablaze, forcing the paddle-wheeler's commander to beach his ship. At the same moment as *Grenade* was stricken, another bomb plunged into HMT *Calvi*, tearing the trawler apart. Two near misses also badly damaged HMT *Polly Johnston*, killing the trawler's 3in. gun crew to a man. The trawler foundered on the way back to Dover, but all crew and embarked troops aboard were rescued.

After the attack, the stricken *Grenade* was pulled clear of the mole by HMT *John Cattling*, so the destroyer sank well clear of the harbour entrance. While some troops held their nerve, others panicked, forcing some officers to brandish their revolvers, to prevent the terrified soldiers from swamping the remaining vessels. For Tennant, controlling operations from the mole, it turned what had been a successful day into an extremely costly one.

On the evening of 30 May, the French destroyer *Bourrasque*, namesake of the class, sank after striking a mine off Nieuwpoort, some 15 miles north-east of Dunkirk. *Bourrasque* sank in minutes, and despite the efforts of nearby ships, over 800 embarked French soldiers and sailors were lost. Many of these were killed by the destroyer's depth charges, which detonated as the ship sank.

Thursday 30 May–Friday 31 May

On Thursday morning, Route X had opened, shortening the voyage by 32 miles, and avoiding the Nieuwpoort coastal batteries. A bonus was that, for two days, the Germans were unaware of this new route. In any case, low cloud and fog forced the Luftwaffe to ground their aircraft until conditions improved. On the ground, the pressure on the pocket also eased off, as the Germans began withdrawing the bulk of their panzer forces. Although the evacuation got off to a slow start that morning, Tennant examined the East Mole for damage suffered from the previous evening's bombing. HMS *Vanquisher* was sent to inspect it, and her commander reported that the battered mole was still useable, with caution. So, Tennant pronounced it open, but limited access to one ship at a time.

Meanwhile, the French *Pas de Calais* Flotilla returned with two destroyers, five sloops and two torpedo boats. These left the harbour by noon, and while most made it to safety, the destroyer *Bourrasque* struck a mine and sank off Nieuwpoort. On Thursday afternoon, a flotilla of French naval trawlers, minesweepers and a tug arrived in Dunkirk to clear debris and evacuate troops, preparing the way for five French troopships, which made the same run that evening. At 0130hrs, that night, one of the escorts, the destroyer *Cyclone*, was torpedoed by an E-boat, S24, which was lying in wait astride Route Y. The explosion sheared off the destroyer's bow but, with help, *Cyclone* managed to reach Dover.

Despite growing frustration and indiscipline among the Allied troops in the port and the beach, the day's evacuation proved highly successful. The well-planned shuttle of small boats out to bigger ones, then on to larger transports and warships lying in the Roads, proved its worth. The total for troops disembarked in Britain from midnight to midnight on Thursday amounted to 53,227 men. Of these, almost half had been lifted off by destroyers and minesweepers.

Dawn on Friday 31 May revealed a beach littered with small boats. It was clear that there was a huge wastage of them, having been cast adrift once the troops were transferred into larger craft. So, Ramsay sent more seamen to Dunkirk to prevent this recurring. The surf and swell had increased in the night though, but Tennant felt beach evacuation would be practicable by the evening. It was just as well, as many of the 'Little Ships' were now available, and their crews were eager to play their part. It was decided that the night evacuation would be carried out along 10 miles of the beach, between Dunkirk and La Panne (De Panne). That day, ground attacks on the Allied perimeter forced it to contract further. By nightfall, the Allies held a 24-mile-long stretch of coast, running from Mardyck just west of Dunkirk to Nieuwpoort. At its deepest point, at Bergues, it was less than 6 miles from the sea. So, the need for this evacuation had become pressing.

On Friday morning, the French ran a regular shuttle of craft along Routes X and Y that evacuated 14,784 French troops. Among them was

Another photograph of HMS *Venomous* (D75) manoeuvring into a berth alongside another V & W destroyer in Dover, on the morning of 31 May. The quadruple 2-pdr 'pom-pom' pictured – one of two mounted in *Venomous* – ran out of ammunition that afternoon during a heavy air attack, while the destroyer was in Dunkirk Roads. In the background the stern of HMS *Whitehall* (D94) can be seen.

Gen. Bouchard, embarked in the torpedo boat *Bouclier*. An early setback to this French-run operation was the loss of the auxiliary transport SS *Aïn el Turk* in the only successful Stuka attack on the harbour that morning. Also sunk in the attack were two French naval trawlers and a tug. That night, at 2201hrs, the destroyer *Siroco* was sunk in a clash with two E-boats on Route Y, and 650 French troops on board were drowned.

Meanwhile, on Friday afternoon, Ramsay ordered the 'Little Ships' gathered in Ramsgate to set out along Route X. The largest of them also towed barges. The aim was for them to begin their work after sunset, at 2055hrs. The beach evacuation wasn't without its problems, and the 'Little Ships' shied away from La Panne, as it was under artillery bombardment. Still, the operation proved successful enough to make it all worthwhile. That evening, Lord Gort embarked in the minesweeper HMS *Hebe*, but later he transferred to a fast motor launch, which reached Dunkirk at dawn on 1 June. In the meantime, larger ships had spent the evening evacuating troops from the East Mole and the harbour. By midnight, the day's tally for troops disembarked on 31 May had reached 64,141 men – the highest total of Operation *Dynamo*. Two thirds of these had been evacuated by British and French warships, rather than the celebrated 'Little Ships'.

The French crewmen of the destroyer *Bourrasque*, as well as embarked soldiers, being rescued off Nieuwpoort by the French torpedo boat *Branlebas*, which was accompanying *Bourrasque* when the destroyer veered from the swept channel and struck a mine. These were some of the lucky ones – over 400 French sailors and soldiers were lost when the destroyer sank.

Saturday 1 June–Sunday 2 June

By Saturday morning, the skies were clear again, and so the Luftwaffe returned in force. The RAF did what they could, flying eight sweeps over Dunkirk, but during the gaps between them the Stukas went unmolested, wreaking havoc. There were five major attacks, the first coming at 0415hrs, half an hour before dawn, and preceding

The paddlewheel steamer SS *Devonia* was built in 1905, and before World War II the ship operated on the River Severn. At the outbreak of war, *Devonia* was requisitioned and converted into HMS *Devonia* (J113), an auxiliary minesweeper. On 30 May, the ship was hit during an air attack while anchored off La Panne and was beached at low tide. The remains of the wreck can still be seen there today.

the RAF's dawn sweep, giving the 40 Stukas a free hand. Lying off the beach at Bray, 6.5 miles east of Dunkirk, the destroyer HMS *Keith*, flagship of R. Adm. Wake-Walker, was bombed and damaged; while off Dunkirk, the destroyer HMS *Basilisk* was crippled.

At 0720hrs, a second wave of 77 Stukas crippled two more destroyers, HMS *Havant* and HMS *Ivanhoe*, and *Keith* was bombed again. The minesweeper HMS *Skipjack* and two tugs were sunk in the same attack. Aboard *Skipjack*, 275 troops were drowned when the ship sank. Later that day, both *Basilisk* and *Havant* had to be scuttled, but *Ivanhoe* made it to Dover, with 56 crewmen dead or wounded.

The third air attack at 1000hrs was made up of 60 He 111 and Do 17 bombers. This time the only fresh victim was the Yangtze river gunboat HMS *Mosquito*, which was crippled and set on fire. *Mosquito* was scuttled later that day. *Keith* was bombed again, and capsized with the loss of 39 crewmen. Some of *Keith*'s crew had been rescued by the tug HMT *St. Abbs*, which was sunk by a Ju 88 in a fourth wave of bombers at 1030hrs, and 100 survivors of the destroyer's crew were killed. During the third attack, the former railway steamer SS *Prague* was also hit in Dunkirk Roads, but the 3,000 French troops aboard were rescued, and *Prague* was eventually beached near Deal.

At 1030hrs, the returning Stukas targeted the French destroyer *Foudroyant*, which was just off Dunkirk harbour. *Foudroyant* was hit three times and capsized, although most of the destroyer's crew were rescued.

C

FRENCH DESTROYER *BOURRASQUE* STRIKING A MINE, THURSDAY 30 MAY 1940

That Thursday afternoon, the French destroyer *Bourrasque* (T41) embarked some 880 French troops at the Félix Faure Quay in Dunkirk harbour. Then, together with other ships of the *Pas de Calais* Flotilla, the ship began the task of ferrying the troops to safety in southern England. *Bourrasque* and three other Allied warships left Dunkirk harbour at 1530hrs, then headed along Route Y. The first part of this route ran towards the north-east, parallel to the French and Belgian coast, before turning north opposite Ostend, towards the English coast. At 1635hrs, this evacuation force came under fire from a German-manned coastal artillery battery outside Nieuwpoort. Capt. De Frigate Fouque increased speed to 25kts, and turned his ship to port, to increase the range from the battery. Inadvertently, though, this led to the ship straying from the Route Y channel, which was regularly swept by Allied minesweepers.

At 1640hrs, *Bourrasque* was rocked by two virtually simultaneous explosions from the ship's port quarter. At first, Fouque thought these were artillery hits, but as the destroyer began listing it was clear they'd struck a mine. The second explosion was probably an internal one. Panic swept through the packed decks of the ship, and hundreds of soldiers jumped overboard, while others were crushed in the rush for the upper deck and the ship's side. *Bourrasque* sank 15 minutes later, taking some 300 troops and 122 crewmen down too. The survivors were rescued by the French torpedo boat *Branlebas*, and two small British vessels, HMT *Ut Prosim* and HMD *Yorkshire Lass*. This shows *Bourrasque* veering away from the gunfire of the German-manned battery, at the moment the mine detonated, under the destroyer's port quarter, level with the mainmast. Close by, trying to guide the destroyer back into the swept channel, is the French torpedo boat *Branlebas*.

HMS *Basilisk* (H11), an A & B class destroyer from Western Approaches Command, joined the evacuation on 31 May. Under Cdr. Maxwell Richmond, the destroyer made two successful trips that day, evacuating 695 men. The following morning, though, *Basilisk* was dive-bombed while lying off the beach, and a bomb wrecked her engine room. A French naval trawler tried to tow *Basilisk* to safety but the ship was hit again in another attack and wrecked. The destroyer was finished off by the destroyer HMS *Whitehall* to prevent its capture.

The SS *Scotia* had left Dunkirk 30 minutes before, with 2,700 French troops embarked, accompanied by the paddlewheel minesweeper HMS *Brighton Queen*. Both ships were bombed and sunk, with the loss of 900 lives. Finally, at 1600hrs, a last wave of nine Stukas appeared, sinking three French minesweepers off the harbour.

It had been a bruising day for the Allies, but in between these ferocious attacks the evacuation continued. The day's tally for 1 June was 61,557 troops, over half of which (35,013) were French. This, though, would be the last major evacuation of Operation *Dynamo*. Before dawn on Sunday, most of the BEF had been evacuated, and only a few detachments remained. Due to the midnight-to-midnight way the troops landed in Britain were recorded, however, the tally would roll on into 2 June. So, the aim on Sunday was to save as many French troops as possible. During the night of June 1–2, though, the E-boats were active again off Route Y, sinking two patrolling naval trawlers and narrowly missing the destroyer HMS *Widgeon*. This lack of targets had finally led to the Kriegsmarine's realization that the Allies were using another evacuation route further to the east.

HMS *Havant* (H32) was a new G, H & I class destroyer, commissioned the previous December. The destroyer made four trips to Dunkirk, rescuing 2,432 troops. This view shows *Havant* entering Dover on 31 May. At 0906hrs on 1 June, with another 500 troops aboard, *Havant* was bombed off Dunkirk, and the ship began flooding. Lt. Cdr. Anthony Burnell-Nugent transferred the troops, but another attack foiled attempts to tow *Havant* home, and the destroyer sank at 1015hrs.

Sunday morning revealed more clear skies and calm seas, and a Dunkirk Roads that was largely devoid of ships. Only the AA cruiser HMS *Calcutta* remained, accompanied by two sloops and two naval trawlers. Ramsay's intention was to concentrate on night-time evacuation, to avoid a repeat of the previous day's losses. For the last remnants of the BEF, though, and for the French, it must have been a depressingly empty vista. Inevitably then, when the Luftwaffe appeared at 1035hrs, *Calcutta* was attacked by Ju 88s, and although the bombs missed, the elderly cruiser was damaged by two near misses. So, mid-afternoon *Calcutta* headed back to Sheerness for repair.

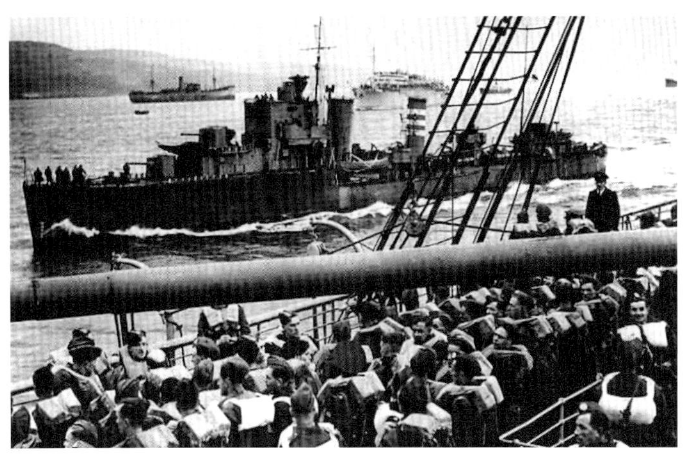

That evening, when the evacuation fleet returned to Dunkirk, the Luftwaffe struck again. At 2015hrs, Stukas crippled the British hospital carrier SS *Paris*, as well as the auxiliary troopship MV *Royal Daffodil*. *Paris* sank the following morning, while *Royal Daffodil* reached Margate before sinking there. An RAF motor launch was also lost in the attack. The rest of Ramsay's force – 11 destroyers, 8 personnel ships, 14 minesweepers and 21 smaller craft – arrived at sunset, followed by a French convoy of 34 fishing boats led by the destroyer *Léopard* and eight smaller warships. In all, 7,208 British troops were rescued, and shortly before midnight, after checking no stragglers could be seen, Capt. Tennant signalled Ramsay in Dover to report: 'Evacuation Complete. Returning to Dover.'

During Operation *Dynamo*, while most troops were embarked from the East Mole, a third were evacuated directly from the beach. For the most part, these were picked up by small boats, then transferred to larger vessels, waiting out in Dunkirk Roads. Here, though, a line of troops approaches a larger personnel ship lying close in to the shore off Malo-les-Bains.

The French rearguard, though, of more than 50,000 men, were still manning Dunkirk's defensive perimeter, or awaiting evacuation. On Monday, mist limited air operations for both sides and, anyway, the bulk of the Luftwaffe were already preparing to support the German drive on Paris. Ramsay sent over everything he could, including his nine remaining serviceable destroyers, as did the French, with the battered *Pas de Calais* Flotilla arriving accompanied by a host of fishing boats. Evacuation took place from both the harbour and the beach, guided by Anglo-French shore parties. The evacuation continued largely uninterrupted, despite several small vessel collisions and groundings.

That evening, the headquarters of French naval forces was closed, and V. Adm. Abrial departed in a French warship. Throughout the day, though, many exhausted French troops abandoned the perimeter and congregated along the beach and East Mole, waiting for rescue. So, the evacuation continued through the night, as German troops reached the outskirts of the port. The crunch came after 0300hrs on 4 June, when the destroyers HMS *Express* and HMS *Shikari* left with 1,000 troops aboard, including

The remains of small French fishing vessels in Dunkirk harbour after the end of the evacuation. These were vessels from French ports on the Channel coast, which had been commandeered to augment French naval trawlers and drifters, in the evacuation of the French First Army from Dunkirk. They were too badly damaged in air attacks to make it home, and so were scuttled in the harbour as the French quit the port.

the small Royal Navy shore party. As *Shikari* backed out, the blockship SS *Pacifico* was scuttled across the harbour mouth, sealing off Dunkirk from the open sea. *Shikari* was the last of Ramsay's ships to leave Dunkirk, but the elderly destroyer wasn't the last casualty. The French naval trawler *Emile Deschamps* struck a mine off the Kent coast and sank with 700 troops aboard. Meanwhile, in Dunkirk, the Germans accepted the surrender of the 40,000-strong French rearguard, who had stayed behind to let their comrades get away. At 1430hrs on 4 June, Operation *Dynamo* was officially declared complete. While the cost to the Allied navies had been high, the British and French troops who made it out would soon be put to work, defending Britain, and taking the war to the enemy in other theatres.

THE BRITISH CONTINGENT

When Operation *Dynamo* was first set in train, on 19 May, V. Adm. Ramsay only had his own Dover Command at his disposal. This was one of several shore commands, each controlling a specific geographical area. The others were Portsmouth, Plymouth and the Nore, augmented at the outbreak of war by Dover, Rosyth and Orkneys and Shetlands commands. In addition, there were two seagoing commands: the Home Fleet, based in Scapa Flow, and Western Approaches, based in Liverpool. The Dover Command had been active during World War I, but had been deactivated during the inter-war years, and reformed again in September 1939, with Ramsay at its head. It existed to protect sea traffic in the Dover Straits, which until then had been part of Nore Command's responsibility. Although Ramsay had a base ship,

THE BRITISH MINESWEEPERS HMS *HALCYON* AND HMS *MEDWAY QUEEN*

In the late 1930s, the ordering of the Halcyon class of 21 modern fleet minesweepers transformed that arm of the fleet. Until then, all of the fleet's existing minesweepers had entered service during or shortly after World War I.

1. HMS *Halycon* (N42 – later J42) HMS *Halycon*, namesake of the class was launched on the Clyde in 1933, and entered service the following April. Officially, *Halcyon* was a 'minesweeping sloop', but during World War II this longer classification dropped from use. While primarily minesweepers, operating in support of the main British fleets, the Halcyons were also used as convoy escorts, and for special minesweeping missions in the North Sea or off the Norwegian coast. Under her commander, Lt. Cdr. John Cox, *Halcyon* formed part of the 4th Minesweeping Flotilla, attached to the Nore Command then, on 26 May 1940, the minesweeper was sent to Dover, to assist in Operation *Dynamo*. From 28 May, though, the flotilla leader Cdr. Eric Hinton assumed direct command of the ship. Between 26 May and 4 June, *Halcyon* made seven trips to Dunkirk and evacuated 2,371 Allied troops. Although subjected to air attacks, the ship emerged unscathed, save for the loss of some of the ship's crew manning a launch, which was strafed while heading towards Dunkirk beach.

2. SS *Medway Queen* (J48) When the war broke out, the Admiralty requisitioned numerous civilian vessels, such as trawlers and merchant ships. These also included a number of paddlewheel steamers, most of which were used as pleasure steamers. All but a handful of these paddle-wheelers were converted and then commissioned into service as auxiliary minesweepers. The SS *Medway Queen* was one of these, a paddle-wheeler built in 1924, to operate in the Thames estuary between Essex and Kent. Requisitioned at the outbreak of war, the paddle-wheeler was converted into a minesweeper, and commissioned as HMS *Medway Queen* (J48). The ship joined the 10th Minesweeping Flotilla, based in Dover, and took part in Operation *Dynamo* from 27 May onwards. HMS *Medway Queen* made seven trips to Dunkirk and evacuated 2,587 Allied troops. Both minesweepers are shown here as they appeared during the Dunkirk operation.

1
2
J48

The destroyer ORP *Błyskawica* (H34), built in Britain for the Polish Navy, and commissioned in 1937. *Błyskawica* ('*Lightning*') escaped to Britain in September 1939, and subsequently served alongside the Royal Navy. During Operation *Dynamo*, under Cdr. Stanislaw Nahorski, the destroyer provided anti-submarine protection off Route Y. *Błyskawica* survived the war, and is now a museum ship in Gdynia.

HMS *Lynx*, his headquarters was housed beneath Dover Castle, in a network of casemates and tunnels.

At the core of Dover Command was a destroyer flotilla of 11 warships, all of which were old destroyers of World War I vintage. These weren't fleet destroyers, of the kind which accompanied the Royal Navy's main fleets, but were ones relegated to secondary tasks, such as convoy escort or anti-submarine sweeps. However, they included a small detachment of three more modern destroyers, one of which was Polish.

Supporting them was a substantial quantity of minesweepers – vital for work in the English Channel. Again, many of these were built during the last war, although a handful were more modern vessels. Also used were a number of Vosper-built motor torpedo boats (MTBs), from a flotilla stationed in Dover, reinforced for *Dynamo* by motor launches culled from other naval commands. These were used to evacuate troops, patrol the shipping routes and act as fast despatch boats. Augmenting the purpose-built minesweepers were a collection of old paddlewheel craft, which had been requisitioned at the start of the war and converted into naval auxiliary vessels. For the most part though, these were used as troop-carrying personnel ships.

The largest component of Dover Command was its naval trawler forces, most of which were used in the anti-submarine or minesweeping roles. Known colloquially as 'Harry Tate's Navy', these sturdy but unglamorous naval auxiliary vessels were true workhorses, crewed largely by former fishermen, and usually commanded by naval reserve officers. Many of these had been commercial fishermen themselves. In Operation *Dynamo*, these were used to recover troops from the beach, acting as a middle link between the smaller boats and the larger vessels lying in Dunkirk Roads. Some were also used to take troops back to Dover. They were also employed to patrol the sea routes between Dover and Dunkirk, to clear mines and as rescue vessels, even though this put them in harm's way.

On 28 May, the A & B class destroyer HMS *Anthony* (H40) evacuated troops from the East Mole, and despite coming under air attack the destroyer reached Dover safely. This was the first of three trips made by *Anthony*, before being damaged on the evening of 30 May, while returning from a fourth trip. Still, the destroyer limped into Dover and unloaded its human cargo. In all, *Anthony* evacuated 3,107 British troops during Operation *Dynamo*.

The naval drifters were similar vessels, albeit usually older and smaller fishing boats, whose usual jobs were to lay danbuoys – temporary navigational markings indicating a mine-free, swept channel, or as boom defence vessels, protecting the entrances to British harbours. They too served as rescue ships off Dunkirk or along the sea routes. Tugs were an important asset for Ramsay, and a handful of Belgian ones, familiar with local waters, were employed in Dunkirk harbour. Most of the British tugs did the same in Dover and other south-coast ports, and in Dunkirk Roads. During the evacuation, they were stationed off the East Mole, to help nudge ships into position, or to evacuate troops themselves.

The old Admiralty S-class destroyer HMS *Scimitar* (H-21) made five trips to Dunkirk, rescuing a total of 2,716 troops. On 31 May *Scimitar* collided with the destroyer *Icarus* off the Goodwin Sands, but completed the last return voyage to Dunkirk with a crumpled bow, which limited the destroyer's speed to just 8–10 knots.

The largest category of naval or naval auxiliary vessels in Ramsay's force were personnel ships, an all-embracing category that included various requisitioned passenger ships such as cross-channel ferries or packets, as well as cargo vessels, coasters and larger passenger ships. These were augmented by smaller naval vessels, such as armed yachts, normally used to protect British harbours and estuaries, or to escort coastal convoys. This category also included 40 Dutch *schuyts* (which the British called 'skoots'). These were wide-beamed and of shallow-draught, predominantly wooden-hulled motor barges, designed for use in shallow Dutch rivers and coastal waters, which varied in length from 50 to 150ft long. For Operation *Dynamo*, they were collected before the Dutch surrender and were manned by Royal Navy crews. These 'skoots' were ideal for the beach evacuation element of *Dynamo*.

Strangely, the category of personnel ships included numerous exotic auxiliary warships. At the start of the war, many smaller passenger vessels, many of them paddle-wheelers, were requisitioned for naval service, and were duly converted into minesweepers. Before the start of *Dynamo*, many of these paddlewheel minesweepers had been attached to the Nore Command, the majority in the 12th Minesweeping Flotilla. There, they regularly swept the waters of the English North Sea coast, or estuaries such as the Thames. A few others were turned into small anti-aircraft ships, to protect British coastal convoys. Although fully-fledged, commissioned Royal Navy warships, they were largely crewed by a mix of naval reservists and merchant seamen. Although some of these odd-looking vessels dated from the end of the previous century, they still proved useful in *Dynamo* as they were well suited to the role of evacuation ships.

The G, H & I class destroyer HMS *Ivanhoe* (D16) arrived off Dunkirk on 28 May, and made the first of four trips to the port. At 0800hrs on 1 June, *Ivanhoe* was attacked by Stukas, and one bomb hit the base of the forward funnel, damaging the forward boiler rooms, killing 23 crewmen and starting a major fire. *Ivanhoe* fought off two more attacks before reaching Sheerness, where the ship underwent six weeks of repairs. During *Dynamo*, *Ivanhoe* evacuated a total of 1,904 troops from Dunkirk.

The personnel ships in *Dynamo* were joined by a small number of hospital carriers (hospital ships), converted from merchantmen, as well as naval storeships, a naval cargo ship, a naval troopship and a handful of naval motor launches. Rounding off the personnel ships were a number of flat-bottomed hopper barges, or

The hospital carrier SS *Isle of Thanet* (Hospital Carrier 22) is pictured alongside the East Mole at Dunkirk. The ship carried a full medical team, and even before Operation *Dynamo* it was being used to evacuate BEF wounded. During *Dynamo*, when these hospital ships came under air attack, Ramsay decided to withdraw them to safety.

Thames sailing barges, which were towed across the Channel to boost capacity.

In addition, Ramsay had the use of 346 smaller craft of various types and sizes – the 'small ships of Dunkirk'. More famously, this motley collection of civilian personnel ships were augmented by 'The Little Ships of Dunkirk'. Even before the crisis facing the BEF, on 14 May, the Admiralty requested 'All owners of self-propelled pleasure craft between 30' and 100' in length to send all particulars to the Admiralty within 14 days'. This was a first step towards the requisition of some 850 small private boats from the rivers and harbours of Southern England. On 27 May, the Ministry of Shipping had these assemble at Ramsgate. Contrary to myth, most weren't manned by their owners, but by naval personnel. Then, they were escorted over to Dunkirk. Ramsay saw their primary role as ferries, transporting troops off the beach, and then taking them out to vessels of larger-draught lying offshore. They proved immensely useful, although few of them were used to transport troops all the way across the Channel.

Dover Command 26 May 1940 (V. Adm. Ramsay)

Destroyers Captain (Destroyers): Capt. Simpson (*Keith*)	
19th Destroyer Flotilla (DF): Capt. Simpson (*Keith*)	*Keith* (flotilla leader), *Basilisk, Verity, Vimiera, Vimy, Whitehall, Whitshed, Wild Swan, Windsor*
1st Destroyer Flotilla (detachment): Capt. Creasy (*Codrington*) Note: *Just arrived from Nore Command – officially attached on 27 May*	*Codrington* (flotilla leader), *Grenade*, ORP *Błyskawica* (Polish Navy)
16th Destroyer Flotilla (detachment): Capt. Halsey (*Malcolm*)	*Malcolm, Mackay, Montrose, Venomous*
Minesweepers	
5th M/S Flotilla: six Hunt-class minesweepers	(*Kellett, Lydd, Pangbourne, Ross, Saltash, Sutton*)
6th M/S Flotilla (detachment): three Halcyon-class minesweepers	(*Harrier, Hebe, Sharpshooter*) anti-submarine patrol vessels
1st Anti-Submarine (A/S) Force: three Kingfisher-class patrol vessels	(*Mallard, Shearwater, Sheldrake*)

In addition, Dover Command contained nine minesweeper armed trawlers in each of M/S Groups 51 and 61, and 12 A/S armed trawlers in A/S Groups 10 and 11.

The 1st Motor Torpedo Boat (MTB) Flotilla of six boats (MTB-6, MTB-67, MTB-68, MTB-100, MTB-102, MTB-107) was based in Dover, but while available to Ramsay, officially it formed part of Coastal Forces Command, based in Harwich. Also available, and attached to the flotilla, were three motor anti-submarine boats (MA/SB-6, MA/SB-7, MA/SB-10).

Reinforcements

From Nore Command	
1 C - class AA cruiser	*Calcutta*, Capt. Lees
1st DF: one destroyer	*Gallant*
20th DF: five minelaying destroyers	*Icarus, Impulsive, Intrepid, Esk, Express*
22nd DF: two destroyers	*Grafton, Greyhound*
Unassigned destroyers	*Shikari, Venetia*
4th M/S Flotilla: two minesweepers	*Halcyon, Salamander*
6th M/S Flotilla: three minesweepers	*Niger, Skipjack, Speedwell*
Thames Estuary Defence Flotilla	Two gunboats (*Locust, Mosquito*)

From Rosyth Command	
Rosyth Escort Force	One destroyer (*Vega*)
5th M/S Flotilla	One minesweeper (*Leda*)
From Western Approaches Command	
11th DF	One destroyer (*Vanquisher*)
16th DF	One destroyer (*Venomous*)
17th DF	Two destroyers (*Vivacious*, *Wakeful*)
Unassigned destroyers	(*Sabre*, *Saladin*, *Whitehall*)
1st Sloop Division:	One sloop (*Bideford*)
From Portsmouth Command	
Portsmouth Flotilla	One destroyer (*Scimitar*)
16th DF	One destroyer (*Anthony*)
From Belgian Navy	Three naval trawlers
	Five civilian tugs (including one rescue tug)
From Dutch Navy	Two armed yachts (prefixed 'HNLMS')
Vessels assigned to Dover Command by Admiralty as personnel ships:	
Naval vessels (36)	Three paddlewheel anti-aircraft ships (prefixed 'HMS')
	21 paddlewheel minesweepers (prefixed 'HMS')
	Six motor lighters (launches) (prefixed 'X')
	Six motor torpedo boats (prefixed 'MTB')
Auxiliary naval vessels (71)	One naval cargo ship (prefixed 'HMS')
	Two armed boarding vessels (prefixed 'HMS')
	20 naval drifters (prefixed 'HMD')
	Ten armed yachts (prefixed HMY')
	24 troopships / transport ships (prefixed 'TS', 'SS' or 'MV')
	Nine naval storeships (prefixed 'SS' or 'MV')
	Eight hospital carriers (prefixed 'SS')
Merchant vessels (100)	Eight cargo ships (prefixed 'SS')
	Three small paddle-steamers (prefixed 'PS')
	Five small ferries (prefixed 'MV')
	Ten coasters (prefixed 'SS' or 'MV')
	Nine trawlers (no prefix)
	Five river ferries (prefixed 'MV')
	One motor barge (no prefix)
	Seven unpowered hopper barges (no prefix)
	Eight Thames sailing barges (no prefix)
	42 Dutch schuyts / 'skoots' (prefixed 'HMS')
Other vessels assigned to Dover Command by Admiralty (45)	30 harbour tugs (prefixed 'HMT' or 'ST')
	Eight rescue tugs (prefixed 'HMT or 'ST')
	Seven blockships (prefixed 'SS')

The auxiliary minesweeper HMS *Queen of Thanet* was commanded by Cdr. Sidney Herival RNVR, senior officer of the 12th Minesweeping (M/S) Flotilla based in Harwich. The paddle-wheeler was built in 1916, and served as a cross-channel ferry based in Southend, before being requisitioned in September 1939 and commissioned into naval service. Along with others in the flotilla, the paddle-wheeler was employed as a personnel ship for Operation *Dynamo*.

British warship losses during Operation Dynamo

Destroyers	*Basilisk*	Sunk 29 May
	Grafton	"
	Grenade	"
	Havant	1 June
	Keith	"
	Wakeful	"
Minesweepers	*Brighton Belle*	28 May
	Brighton Queen	
	Gracie Fields	"
	Waverley	29 May
	Devonia	31 May
	Skipjack	1 June
AA ships	*Crested Eagle*	29 May
Gunboats	*Mosquito*	1 June
Armed boarding vessels	*King Orry*	30 May
Armed trawlers	*Thomas Bartlett*	28 May
	Calvi	29 May
	Comfort	"
	Nautilus	"
	Polly Johnson	"
	Thuringia	"
	Argyllshire	1 June
	Stella Dorado	"
	Blackburn Rovers	2 June
	Westella	"
Naval drifters	*Boy Roy*	28 May
	Paton	"
	Girl Pamela	29 June
	Lord Cavan	
Armed yachts	*Amulree*	1 June
	Grive	"

THE FRENCH CONTINGENT

In 1940, the French Navy was divided between several administrative districts and fleets, with the bulk of its ships concentrated in Toulon and Brest. Dunkirk, as the headquarters of *Forces Maritime du Nord* (Naval Forces, North), was one of these. Its administrative boundaries extended from the Cherbourg peninsula in the west to the Belgian border, 10 miles to the east. Its principal military role was the protection of French shipping through *La Manche* (the English Channel), the defence of the French coast from amphibious attack. If required, it would also support French military operations along the coast of the Low Countries – a task the command had performed during World War I.

French troops, packed onto the upper deck of a French personnel ship, most probably the passenger ship *Rouen*, which made three runs to Dunkirk as part of the French coastal convoy, and evacuated 2,404 troops.

In May 1940, the 'Commander-in-Chief of French Naval Forces in the North' was *Vice Amiral* ('Vice Admiral') Jean-Marie Abrial,

Of all the smaller warships employed in Operation *Dynamo*, the most numerous were the naval tugs, trawlers and drift drawlers, requisitioned into naval service at the outbreak of war. Here, the French rescue tug *Lutteur* (foreground, left) heads towards Dunkirk, followed by a French naval trawler, possibly the *Président Briand*. Heading away from Dunkirk is a small group of British-flagged personnel ships – in this case small coasters, like the one pictured off the tug's beam.

whose official title was usually abbreviated to 'Admiral Nord'. He had held the post since December 1939, and so was familiar with the theatre and the naval forces under his command. As an ally of the British, Abrial had worked closely with his Royal Navy counterparts, as together they shared another strategic role – the blocking of the *Pas de Calais* to German naval forces. Fortunately, Abrial and Ramsay worked well together. In the event of a German invasion of the Low Countries, the military plan called for Anglo-French forces to advance into Belgium and even send an expeditionary force to Vlissingen in the Netherlands. So, Abrial was given the forces he needed to ensure he could support either operation if required. After the German invasion of 10 May, though, the military situation quickly deteriorated, and these allied forces began their retreat towards Dunkirk.

Although Abrial's military superior, General Weygrand, was informed of British preparations for a naval evacuation as early as 20 May 1940, Abrial was taken unawares by Operation *Dynamo*. Fortunately, he had already gathered his own evacuation force, in case it was needed to extricate French troops from ports on *La Manche*. This was achieved by requisitioning suitable vessels from within his naval district. The bulk of these were assembled at Rouen. Further west, similar preparations were taking place in Brest and Cherbourg, using ships and stores earmarked for transport to Norway, where French forces were still fighting. On 19 May, though, the Luftwaffe mined the Seine estuary, precluding the immediate use of Le Havre or Rouen as assembly areas. Eventually, however, 37 suitable ships were requisitioned as personnel vessels.

The main fighting element of Abrial's force was the *Pas de Calais* Flotilla, based at Dunkirk, whose destroyers played a prominent part in the forlorn defence of Boulogne and Calais, 22–26 May. One of these ships, the destroyer *Orage*, was lost, and several others damaged. For *Dynamo*, Abrial had seven operational destroyers available, three of which were the 'super-destroyers' favoured by the French in the 1920s. These were supported by a small flotilla of four minesweepers and two sloops, used for mine clearance and anti-submarine patrols respectively, in the *Pas de Calais*. During Operation *Dynamo*, these destroyers would be used as escort vessels for Abrial's convoys, while also serving as high-speed evacuation transports when required.

In addition, Admiral Nord commanded a force of 23 naval armed trawlers and five naval drifters. Most of the trawlers were used as auxiliary

A view of HMS *Havant* entering Dover on the afternoon 31 May, passing the French fleet *Commandant Delage* (A12). The British destroyer landed 932 men at 1720hrs, before spending the evening alongside. *Havant* left for Dunkirk well before dawn the following morning and was hit in an air attack. The bodies of six of *Havant*'s crew were never recovered.

minesweepers. These were augmented by ten requisitioned civilian trawlers, to form small-ship evacuation convoys during the closing days of *Dynamo*. The bulk of Abrial's evacuation capacity, though, lay in the 21 personnel vessels at his disposal, merchant ships of various types. Most of these ranged in size from 500 to 3,250 tons, although two cargo ships were larger – SS *Aden* (8,000 tons) and *Saint Octave* (5,000 tons) – as was the tanker *Salomé* (13,400 tons). Abrial was reluctant to risk his cargo ships, though, and most only made one attempted evacuation, which was cancelled due to improving weather conditions – and the reluctance of many French masters to risk their requisitioned ships.

When Operation *Dynamo* got under way, Abrial organized his own relief convoy to evacuate French wounded from Dunkirk. He also worked closely with Capt. Tennant, Ramsay's 'man on the ground' in Dunkirk, to ensure subsequent French convoys formed part of *Dynamo*, eventually switching his destination port for evacuated French troops to Dover or other nearby English harbours. Instead of cargo ships, Abrial made use of his faster passenger ships, particularly the modern *Côte d'Argent* (3,047 tons) and the older *Newhaven*, a cross-channel ferry (1,881 tons), which made five and three trips to Dunkirk respectively, evacuating a total of 6,933 French troops. After 30 May, though, Abrial largely relied on his fleet of trawlers to carry out evacuations, along with his smaller warships. This continued until the closing down of the French naval headquarters in Dunkirk on 3 May.

E

THE FRENCH DESTROYERS *LÉOPARD* AND *ÉPERVIER*

In the 1920s, the French began designing a new type of 'super-destroyer', although they still called these warships *contre-torpilleurs* (torpedo-boat destroyers). These were in response to the large flotilla leaders built by the British and German navies during World War I.

1. *Léopard* (X22). *Léopard* (X22) was one of the first of these, one of six destroyers of the Chacal class. The ship was launched in St-Nazaire in 1924, and entered service three years later. The Chacals were well-armed, with a main armament of 5.1in. (130mm) guns, as well as six torpedoes. During the mid-1930s, *Léopard* spent some time as a cadet training ship, but at the outbreak of war the ship was assigned to escort duties, protecting convoys sailing between Brest and French North Africa. Then, in May, *Léopard* was assigned to the *Pas de Calais* Flotilla and, under the command of Capt. Loisel, was involved in supporting both the Boulogne and Dunkirk evacuations. Although *Léopard* didn't evacuate troops from Dunkirk, as the ship was used in an escort role, the *contre-torpilleur* did rescue 19 British troops found adrift in a small boat, and delivered them safely to Dover. This shows the appearance of *Léopard* when first assigned to the flotilla.

2. *Épervier* (X112). *Épervier* was one of six Aigle-class 'super-destroyers' – enlarged and improved versions of the Chacal and Guépard classes that preceded them. These mounted more powerful and faster-firing 5.46in. (138.6mm) guns – an armament which was almost the equivalent of a light cruiser. *Épervier* was launched in Lorient in 1931, and entered service in 1934. Like *Léopard*, in the aftermath of the German invasion the big *contre-torpilleur* was assigned to the *Pas de Calais* Flotilla, and during Operation *Dynamo*, *Épervier* was used as close-escort for French troopships, evacuating soldiers from Dunkirk harbour. Although attacked several times, and unlike many other destroyers from the flotilla, *Épervier* came through *Dynamo* largely unscathed. Like *Léopard*, *Épervier* lacked a camouflage scheme at this stage of the war, and the *contre-torpilleur* appeared as shown here.

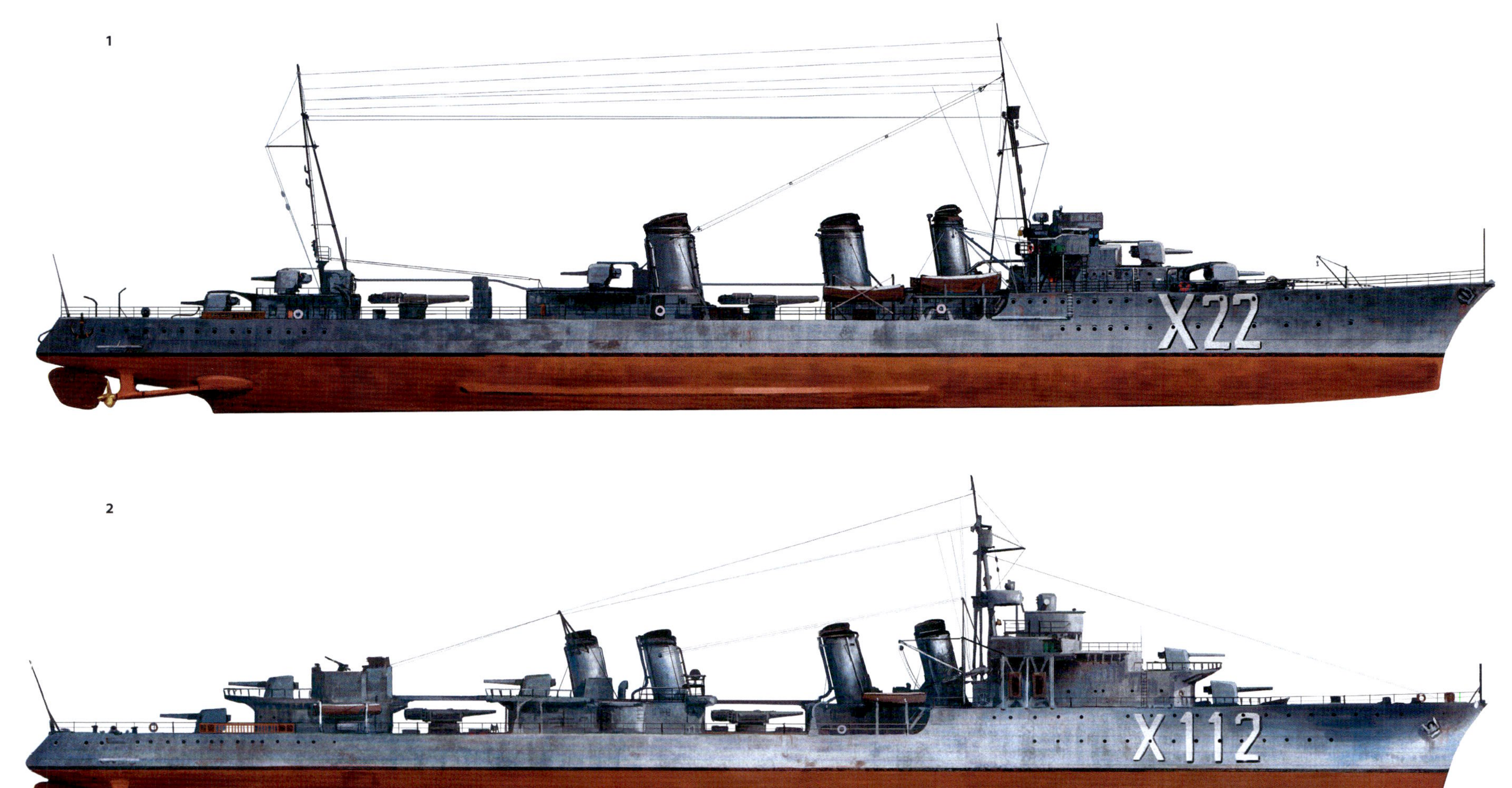
1
X22
2
X112

Forces Maritime du Nord 26 May 1940 (V. Adm. Abrial)	
Pas de Calais Flotilla	Seven destroyers (*Bourrasque, Cyclone, Épervier, Foudroyant, Léopard, Mistral, Siroco*)
	Three sloops (*Arras, Belfort, Savorgnan de Brazza*)
	Four minesweepers (*Commandant Delage, Commandant Riviere, L'Impéteuse, La Boudeuse*)
	torpedo boats (*Bouclier, Branlebas, La Flore, L'Incomprise*)
	One gunboat (*Diligente*)
Auxiliary naval vessels supporting the flotilla consisted of 23 armed trawlers and four naval drifters, a dredger, three harbour tugs and a rescue tug. Also available to the Nord Command were two auxiliary naval patrol vessels, the former cargo ships, *Cérons* and *Sauternes*, which were used to augment the French personnel ships.	
Personnel ships available to Admiral Nord	Two naval cargo ships (*Cérons, Sauternes*)
	23 naval trawlers
	13 cargo ships
	Five passenger ships
	Ten civilian trawlers

French warship losses during Operation Dynamo		
Destroyers	*Bourrasque*	30 May
	Foudroyant	1 June
	Marguerite Rose	26 May
Naval trawlers	*Emma*	29 May
	Denis Papan	1 June
	Emile Deschamps	4 June

WARSHIPS IN ACTION

When ordered to Dunkirk, the crews of some Royal Navy crews saw the evacuation as a break from the routine of escorting convoys. Some warships though, had already been involved in evacuations from Dutch and Norwegian ports, and so their crews knew what was expected of them.

Aboard the destroyer flotilla leader, HMS *Keith*, Gunner Nethercott remembered his first glimpse of Dunkirk on 28 May:

> It was quite obvious where Dunkirk was. Huge clouds of black smoke obscured the coast, and the rolling thunder of gunfire drowned out the throbbing sound of our engines. At frequent intervals we passed other destroyers and sloops belting back towards British ports, through moderately choppy seas, heavily-laden with masses of soldiers crammed in and on every conceivable space.

When a low-flying Heinkel He 111 bomber came towards them, the order was given to open fire:

> 'Soapy' Hudson the gunlayer on the starboard 'pom-pom' obeyed with alacrity. The new 3-inch high-angle gun crew got away a couple of wild shots, but 'Soapy' was close enough to the German's nose section to make the twin-engined bomber bank steeply and roar away to seek an easier target.

Embarking troops from the East Mole greatly sped up the process, particularly at high tide, when the soldiers could more easily clamber aboard the waiting ships. Here, men of the BEF begin boarding the Hunt-class minesweeper HMS *Kellet* (J05) on the afternoon of 28 May, as the vessel lay along the inner side of the mole. The minesweeper made five runs to Dunkirk, taking off 1,446 Allied troops.

> *Keith* then entered Dunkirk harbour. The quays were an utter shambles. The troops were marched along the mole ... to the embarkation points onto waiting destroyers and sloops. We had normal gangplanks over to the mole, but had to station our sailors on the planks to prevent the exhausted soldiers from overbalancing and toppling into the sea below. Our ship's cook worked miracles in the galley – large mess kettles full of piping-hot soup and huge wads of corned beef sandwiches.

Like many of her type, the old Admiralty W-class destroyer HMS *Verity* (D63) was earmarked for conversion into a long-range convoy escort, but in 1940 the ship looked much as she did when first commissioned in 1919. On 28–29 May, *Verity* was damaged by fire from shore batteries and from near-misses by bombs, but managed to rescue 504 British troops. On 30 May, though, morale problems led to Ramsay holding the destroyer in Dover for the remainder of the evacuation.

Many of the troops, though, were too tired to eat, and fell asleep where they were, having absolute confidence that the Navy would look after them.

On 29 May, the auxiliary AA paddle-wheeler HMS *Crested Eagle* came under air attack while lying alongside the same spot on the East Mole. At 1700hrs, the troopship SS *Fenella* was hit next to the vessel by a bomb which dropped down a funnel. As the ship sank, *Crested Eagle* took on survivors, then returned to the task of embarking troops from the mole. Once full, the paddle-wheeler swung clear, but minutes later the ship came under air attack.

Corporal Carman, a signaller from III Corps headquarters, was one of the troops below decks:

> The boat finally sailed, and had been underway for about ten minutes when we heard a stick of bombs coming. We knew they were ours and dropped flat. A second later a bomb seemed to burst right on the ship's bottom. The lights went out, and there was a scorching blast of hot air. Then the room filled with choking fumes and smoke as though from the wrecked funnel. The boat kept going, and was run aground in shallow water.

In his report, *Crested Eagle*'s commander, Lt. Cdr. Booth RNR, wrote:

> As I learned afterwards, five bombs were dropped together, four of which hit the ship. As the engines (paddles) were still working, I held on my course for a while, but I soon discovered the ship was on fire, from amidships aft ... [Booth decided to run his ship onto the beach. Once aground ...] Fire steadily gained ground ... and in very few minutes was on fire fore and aft ... As the lower decks filled first, casualties from the bomb explosions must have been severe.

An S30 type S-boat putting to sea from Ostend, at the start of a patrol in the English Channel. During Operation *Dynamo*, S-boats (known as E-boats by the British), based in the Dutch port of Vlissingen on the Schelde estuary, successfully ambushed British ships passing along Route Y, where S30 sank the destroyer HMS *Wakeful*. Each of these E-boats carried a pair of 21in. (53.3cm) G7 torpedoes.

Carman, of course, was right there:

> There was a first blind rush for the one stairway, and a fight to get out, until someone started singing 'Roll out the Barrel', and amazingly it had the effect of bringing common-sense to bear. It wasn't long before we were all climbing out, only to find ourselves in another saloon, now well alight. However, an axe was found by the sailors, and through an aperture we clambered – to find planes still overhead, and the sea dotted with men.

The rescue of British troops by the crew of the minesweeper HMS *Lydd* (N44), after the French naval trawler they had embarked in was sunk in an air attack off Dunkirk beach on 1 June. This was all too commonplace during *Dynamo*, with numerous smaller boats being lost, through damage suffered during air attacks.

Sure enough, Booth had given the order to abandon ship, and about 200 men made it to safety, despite some being strafed while in the water. Although the number of troops aboard wasn't recorded, probably others – mainly troops – lost their lives in the attack.

As well as the Luftwaffe, the Kriegsmarine also posed a threat, as E-boats and at least one U-boat lay in wait astride Route Y, near the Kwint Buoy. Gunner Nethercott described the threat posed while returning from Dunkirk, laden with troops:

> Inevitably we were all getting very tired, as we could only 'cat-nap' beside our guns at night because of the very real danger of German E-boats which would creep into the area at night. During the early hours of 29 May, one E-boat had already sunk the destroyer *Wakeful*. She was packed with soldiers at the time. Her sinking was a terrible tragedy, with all those soldiers drowned below decks.... So much for Hitler's 'Chivalrous Legions'.

Cdr. Fisher, commanding the destroyer HMS *Wakeful*, reported that when steaming along Route Y, all gun crews were closed up at action stations:

> At 0045 (Wednesday 29 May) when the ship was two cables [400 yards] west of Kwint Buoy, two parallel torpedo tracks about 30 yards apart ... were seen approaching on the starboard bow ... the tracks were practically on the surface, and were very bright with phosphorescence.

THE DESTROYER HMS *WAKEFUL* UNDER ATTACK FROM E-BOAT S30, WEDNESDAY 29 MAY 1940

On Tuesday afternoon, the World War I vintage destroyer HMS *Wakeful* embarked 640 troops while lying off the beach to the east of Dunkirk. Then, at 2300hrs, the destroyer weighed and steamed off to the east along Route Y. Following astern were the destroyer HMS *Grafton* and two minesweepers (*Gossamer* and *Lydd*). Unknown to the British, three German S-boats (E-boats) of the 2nd *Schnellbootsflotilla* also left Vlissingen (Flushing) on the Dutch coast, to lay an ambush along the Allied evacuation route. The spot chosen by S30 was the Kwint Buoy, a navigational marker 12 miles off Ostend.

As *Wakeful* approached the buoy, the destroyer was ahead of the others, making 20kts, and 'zig-zagging'. At 0045hrs, S30 launched two torpedoes. On *Wakeful*'s open bridge, Lt. Cdr. Fisher spotted them and turned his destroyer hard to port. He avoided the first torpedo, but the second slammed into the destroyer's starboard side. The explosion cut *Wakeful* in two, the ship sank in just 15 seconds. Only four soldiers and 25 of the destroyer's crew survived.

This shows the attack by Oberleutnant zur See Zimmerman's E-boat, S30. The torpedoes were launched at a range of 600m, set to run shallow, 25m apart. Their phosphorescent wake was spotted on *Wakeful*'s bridge, where Fisher gave his order to turn. It was too late, though, and the second torpedo struck the destroyer abreast the engine room, ripping the vessel in two. By then, Zimmerman was heading away into the darkness. Meanwhile, half a mile astern of *Wakeful*, the minesweeper HMS *Gossamer* is shown approaching the stricken destroyer, followed by HMS *Lydd*.

Fisher ordered the wheel turned hard over, and they avoided one torpedo, which was slightly ahead of the other. Then:

> The other hit in the forward boiler room. The ship broke apart, and the two portions sank within about 15 seconds, each remaining standing with its midships end on the bottom, and the bow and stern standing 60ft above the surface. Most of the gun crews floated clear. All the troops were asleep below, and went down with the ship, except one, and all of HMS *Wakeful*'s engineering department except one or two were lost.

Shortly afterwards, two drifters began rescuing survivors, and were soon joined by the minesweeper HMS *Gossamer*. In his report, Cdr. Ross, commanding *Gossamer*, described coming across the aftermath of the attack while returning from Dunkirk with 420 men aboard:

> Proceeding towards Kwint Buoy, we soon came into a patch of water filled with men crying 'Help!', and heads could be seen all around in the sea. I stopped and lowered boats. I was then hailed by Cdr. Fisher of HMS *Wakeful*, who said he had been torpedoed, and that the submarine was still nearby. In actual fact I think he was attacked by an E-Boat. But, my boats and almost all my officers were lost in the night, and it took some time to recover them with such few men as they had been able to pick up ... No doubt we were wrong to stop, but at the time I thought otherwise.

At Dunkirk, the most effective weapon in the Royal Navy's woefully inadequate anti-aircraft arsenal was the 2-pdr (1.57in. or 40mm) 'Pom-Pom'. First developed in 1915, this belt-fed automatic AA gun had an effective range of a little over a mile, and a rate of fire of around 60rpm. It proved prone to jams and stoppages, though, at least until the multi-barrelled Mark VIII version entered service, which used metal clips rather than woven ammunition belts.

When the evacuation ended, the last destroyer to leave Dunkirk was HMS *Shikari*. However, the last British warship to quit the port was a tiny Thornycroft MTB, under of the command of Lt. Cameron RNVR. Later, he recalled the experience:

> The flames over the city didn't seem as fierce as the night before, but the pall of smoke, which none who saw could ever forget, still streamed westward from the dying town, and the ring of gun flashes had closed in an ever-narrowing semicircle. It was plain the end couldn't now be far off.

Cameron's job was to take the crew off the blockship, which was to seal the harbour entrance. The blockship, though, began sinking early, after detonating a stray mine, and MTB-107 began rescuing the crew from the water. A reserve blockship duly completed the task.

Cameron then left the harbour and, as he went, he took a last look around:

> The scene was one of tragedy and desolation. Silent and deserted wrecks, a few French fishing craft, a black and huddled line of Frenchmen waiting hopelessly on the eastern jetty. We could do nothing for them, but it felt rather like desertion to leave them there. Outside again [there were] more wrecks – the charred and blackened remains of many ships. The whole scene was filled with a sense of finality and death – the curtain was ringing down on a great tragedy.

On the afternoon of 28 May, HMS *Wakeful* (H88) left Dunkirk with 640 BEF troops aboard and sailed for Dover along Route Y. At 0045hrs the following morning, *Wakeful* was torpedoed by a German E-boat, S30, which had been lying in wait. Only four of the soldiers and 25 crewmen survived the sinking.

MTB-107 and its 20-man crew made it safely back to Dover that morning, at 0730hrs.

WARSHIP SPECIFICATIONS

Royal Navy*

Cruisers

C class (Carlisle group) | HMS *Calcutta* (D82) | Anti-Aircraft Cruiser

Displacement:	5,250 tons (fully laden)		
Commissioned:	1919 (Re-commissioned as AA cruiser 1939)		
Dimensions:	Length overall: 451′ 6″ (137.6m), Beam: 43′ 6″ (13.3m), Draught: 14′ 3″ (4.34m)		
Propulsion:	Two shafts, two turbines, six boilers	Max speed:	29 knots
Armament:	Eight 4″ (102mm) guns in four twin mounts, four 2-pdr (40mm) 'pom-pom' AA guns in single quadruple mount, eight 0.5″ (13.25mm) machine guns in two quadruple mountings	Complement:	350
Armour:	3″ (76mm) belt, 1 ½–2 ¼″ (38–57mm) at bow and stern, 1″ (25mm) deck		

Destroyers

Scott class | HMS *Malcolm* (D19), HMS *Mackay* (D70), HMS *Montrose* (D01)

Displacement:	2,050 tons (fully laden)	Commissioned:	1918–19
Dimensions:	Length overall: 332′ 6″ (101.3m), Beam: 31′ 9″ (9.64m), Draught: 12′ 6″ (3.8m)		
Propulsion:	Two shafts, two turbines, four boilers	Max speed:	36 knots
Armament:	Five 4.7″ (120mm) guns in single mounts, one 3″ (75mm) AA gun in single mount, two 2-pdr (40mm) 'pom-pom' AA guns in single mounts, six 21 (53.3cm) torpedoes in two triple launchers	Complement:	183

V class | HMS *Vanquisher* (D54), HMS *Vega* (L41), HMS *Vivacious* (D36)

Displacement:	1,490 tons (fully laden)	Commissioned	1918–19
Dimensions:	Length overall: 312′ (95.13m), Beam: 29′ 6″ (9m), Draught: 10′ 6″ (3.2m)		
Propulsion:	Two shafts, two turbines, three boilers	Max speed:	34 knots
Armament:	Five 4″ (102mm) guns in single mounts, one 3″ (75mm) AA gun in single mount, four 21 (53.3cm) torpedoes in two twin launchers	Complement:	134

W class | HMS *Wakeful* (L91)

Displacement:	1,490 tons (fully laden)	Commissioned:	1918–19
Dimensions:	Length overall: 312′ (95.13m), Beam: 29′ 6″ (9m), Draught: 10′ 6″ (3.2m)		

Note: *ft is denoted by ′ and in. by ″ within the tables.*

The disembarkation of BEF troops at Dover from the stern of an old V & W class destroyer of the 19th Destroyer Flotilla (DF). These warships of World War I vintage came into their own during Operation *Dynamo*, especially after 1 June, when losses to his more modern destroyers prompted Ramsay to withdraw them from the operation.

British soldiers coming ashore in Dover, over the decks of a pair of V & W class destroyers, after their evacuation from Dunkirk on 1 June. The inboard destroyer on the left of the photograph is probably HMS *Whitehall* (D94), armed with single 2-pdr guns amidships, while the outboard destroyer, possibly HMS *Vimy* (D33), has a four-barrelled 0.5in. machine gun mount in the same position. Together they rescued 5,749 Allied troops.

Propulsion:	Two shafts, two turbines, three boilers	Max speed:	34 knots
Armament:	Four 4" (102mm) guns in single mounts, one 3" (75mm) AA gun in single mount, six 21" (53.3cm) torpedoes in two triple launchers	Complement:	134

S class (Admiralty version) | HMS *Scimitar* (H21), HMS *Saladin* (H54), HMS *Shikari* (D85), HMS *Sabre* (H18)

Displacement:	1,220 tons (fully laden)	Commissioned:	1919–20
Dimensions:	Length overall: 276' (84.1m), Beam: 26' 8" (8.1m), Draught: 9' (2.7m)		
Propulsion:	Two shafts, two turbines, three boilers.	Max speed:	36 knots
Armament:	Three 4" (102mm) guns in single mounts, one 2pdr (40mm) 'pom-pom' AA gun in single mount, four 21" (53.3cm) torpedoes in two twin launchers	Complement:	90

Modified W class | HMS *Vimy* (D33), HMS *Verity* (D63), HMS *Venomous* (D75), HMS *Whitehall* (D94), HMS *Whitshed* (D77)

Displacement:	1,508 tons (fully laden)	Commissioned	1919–20
Dimensions:	Length overall: 312' (95.13m), Beam: 29' 6" (9m), Draught: 10' 6" (3.2m)		
Propulsion:	Two shafts, two turbines, three boilers	Max speed:	34 knots
Armament:	Four 4.7" (120mm) guns in single mounts, one 3" (75mm) AA gun in single mount, two 2-pdr (40mm) 'pom-pom' AA guns in single mounts, six 21" (53.3cm) torpedoes in two triple launchers	Complement:	127

A & B class | HMS *Anthony* (H40), HMS *Basilisk* (H11), HMS *Keith* (D06), HMS *Codrington* (D82) – flotilla leaders

Displacement:	1,930 tons (fully laden). *Keith* 1,990 tons, *Codrington* 2,012 tons	Commissioned:	1930–31
Dimensions:	Length overall: 323' (98.45m) *Codrington*: 343' (104.54m), Beam: 32' 3" (9.64m) *Codrington* 33' 9' (10.29m), Draught: 12' 8" (3.86m)		
Propulsion:	Two shafts, two turbines, four boilers	Max speed:	35¼ knots
Armament:	Four 4.7" (120mm) guns in single mounts (five guns in *Codrington*), two 2-pdr (40mm) 'pom-pom' AA guns in single mounts, eight 21" (53.3cm) torpedoes in two quadruple launchers	Complement:	138 (*Keith*: 175, *Codrington*: 185)

E & F class | HMS *Esk* (H15), HMS *Express* (H67)

Displacement:	1,940 tons (fully laden)	Commissioned:	1935
Dimensions:	Length overall: 329' (100.28m), Beam: 33' 3" (10.13m), Draught: 12' 6" (3.81m)		
Propulsion:	Two shafts, two turbines, four boilers	Max speed:	36 knots
Armament:	Four 4.7" (120mm) guns in single mounts, four 0.5" (13.25mm) machine guns in single quadruple mount, eight 21" (53.3cm) torpedoes in two quadruple launchers	Complement:	145

G, H & I class | HMS *Gallant* (H59), HMS *Grafton* (H89), HMS *Grenade* (H86), HMS *Greyhound* (H89), HMS *Harvester* (H19), HMS *Havant* (H32), HMS *Icarus* (D03), HMS *Impulsive* (D11), HMS *Intrepid* (D10)

Displacement:	1,890 tons (fully laden); *Harvester*, *Havant*: 2,020 tons)		
Commissioned:	1936–38 (*Harvester, Havant*: 1940)		
Dimensions:	Length overall: 323' (98.45m), Beam: 33' (10.06m), Draught: 13' 1" (3.99m)		
Propulsion:	Two shafts, two turbines, four boilers	Max speed:	35–36 knots
Armament:	Four 4.7" (120mm) guns in single mounts (three guns in *Harvester, Havant),* four 0.5" (13.25mm) machine guns in single quadruple mount, eight 21" (53.3cm) torpedoes in two quadruple launchers	Complement:	145

Note: *Harvester* and *Havant* were built for the Brazilian Navy, then brought into service in 1939, while still fitting out.

Grom class | ORP *Błyskawica* (H34) – Polish Navy (in exile) – operating with Royal Navy

Displacement:	3,383 tons (fully laden)	Commissioned:	1937
Dimensions:	Length overall: 374' (114m), Beam: 36' 1" (11m), Draught: 10' 10" (3.3m)		
Propulsion:	Two shafts, two turbines, four boilers	Max speed:	39 knots
Armament:	Seven 4.7" (120mm) Bofors guns in three twin and one single mount, four 40mm Bofors AA guns in two twin mounts, eight 0.3" (13.25mm) machine guns in two quadruple mounts, six 22" (55cm) torpedoes in two triple launchers	Complement:	180

Minesweepers

Hunt class | HMS *Albury* (J41), HMS *Dundalk* (J60), MS *Fitzroy* (J03), HMS *Kellett* (J05), HMS *Lydd* (J44), HMS *Pangbourne* (J37), HMS *Ross* (J45), HMS *Saltash* (J62), HMS *Sutton* (J78)

Displacement:	750 tons (standard)	Commissioned:	1918–19
Dimensions:	Length overall: 231′ (70.4m), Beam: 28′ (8.5m), Draught: 7′ (2.1m)		
Propulsion:	Two shafts, two reciprocating steam engines, two boilers	Max speed:	16 knots
Armament:	One 4″ (102mm) gun in single mount, one 12pdr (3″ or 76mm) AA gun on single mount, two 0.303″ (7.7mm) machine guns in single twin mounting	Complement:	71

Halcyon class | HMS *Gossamer* (J63), HMS *Halcyon* (J42), HMS *Hebe* (J24), HMS *Leda* (J93), HMS *Niger* (J73), HMS *Salamander* (J86), HMS *Sharpshooter* (J68) HMS *Skipjack* (J38), HMS *Speedwell* (J87)

Displacement:	1,330 tons (fully laden)	Commissioned:	1938–39
Dimensions:	Length overall: 245′ 6″ (74.83m), Beam: 33′ 6″ (10.21m), Draught: 10′ 3″ (3.12m)		
Propulsion:	Two shafts, two turbines, two boilers	Max speed:	17 knots
Armament:	Two 4″ (102mm) guns in single mounts, four 0.5″ (13.2mm) machine guns in single quadruple mounting	Complement:	80

Sloops

Shoreham class | HMS *Bideford* (L43)

Displacement:	1,590 tons (fully laden)	Commissioned:	1932
Dimensions:	Length overall: 281′ 4″ (85.75m), Beam: 35′ (10.67m), Draught: 10′ 6″ (3.2m)		
Propulsion:	Two shafts, two turbines, two boilers	Max speed:	16½ knots
Armament:	Two 4″ (102mm) guns in single mounts, four 0.5″ (13.5mm) machine guns in single quadruple mounting	Complement:	100

Patrol vessels

Kingfisher class | HMS *Mallard* (L42), HMS *Shearwater* (L39), HMS *Sheldrake* (L06)

Displacement:	740 tons (fully laden), *Shearwater* 790 tons	Commissioned:	1938–40
Dimensions:	Length overall: 243′ 3″ (74.14m), *Shearwater*: Length: 233′ 3″ (71.09m), Beam: 26′ 6″ (8.08m); *Shearwater:* Draught: 25′ 6″ (7.77m)		
Draught:	8′ (244m). Shearwater 8′ 9″ (2.67m)		
Propulsion:	Two shafts, two turbines, two boilers	Max speed:	20 knots
Armament:	One 4″ (102mm) guns in single mount, two 2-pdr (40mm) 'pom-pom' AA guns in single twin mounting. *Shearwater* also mounted a 12-pdr (3″ or 76mm) AA gun on single mount	Complement:	60

The Halcyon-class minesweeper HMS *Hebe* (J24) embarked Lord Gort, commander of the BEF, on the evening of 30 May, collecting him by boat from the beach near La Panne. Lt. Cdr. John Temple's minesweeper was then subjected to a ferocious air attack, but by manoeuvring at speed it dodged the bombs, before handing Lord Gort over to the destroyer HMS *Keith*. *Hebe* then embarked 420 troops from the beach before heading back to Dover.

River gunboats

Dragonfly class | HMS *Locust* (T28), HMS *Mosquito* (T94) | Built for colonial service

Displacement:	1,715 tons (fully laden)	Commissioned:	1940
Dimensions:	Length overall: 196′ 6″ (59.89m), Beam: 33′ 8″ (10.26m), Draught: 6′ 2″ (1.88m)		
Propulsion:	Two shafts, two turbines, two boilers	Max speed:	17 knots
Armament:	Two 4″ (102mm) guns in single mounts, four 2-pdr (40mm) 'pom-pom' AA guns in single quadruple mounting, eight 0.5″ (13.5mm) machine guns in two quadruple mountings	Complement:	74

Smaller auxiliary vessels

Armed trawlers (42)

Vessel	Displacement (tons) – standard	Completed
HMT *Arctic Pioneer* (FY164)	501	1938
HMT *Argyllshire* (H145)*	540	1940
HMT *Arley* (FY620)	340	1915
HMT *Blackburn Rovers* (FY116)*	422	1934
HMT *Brock* (FY621)	304	1912
HMT *Calvi* (FY715)*	363	1930
HMT *Cayton Wyke* (FY191)	373	1932
HMT *Clyth Ness* (FY1596)	276	1920
HMT *Evelyn Rose* (GY9)	327	1918
HMT *Fyldea* (FY666)	377	1930
HMT *Gava* (FY164)	257	1920
HMT *Grimsby Town* (FY125)	419	1934
HMT *Inverforth* (FY729)	248	1914
HMT *Jacinta* (FD235)	289	1915

Paddle minesweepers (17)

Vessel	Displacement (tons) – standard	Completed
HMS *Brighton Belle* (J117)*	396	1900
HMS *Brighton Queen* (J28)*	807	1905
HMS *Devonia* (J113)*	622	1905
HMS *Duchess of Fife* (J115)	336	1903
HMS *Emperor of India* (J106)	482	1906
HMS *Glen Avon* (J104)	509	1912
HMS *Glen Gower* (J16)	553	1922
HMS *Gracie Fields* (J100)*	393	1936
HMS *Marmion* (J114)	409	1906
HMS *Medway Queen* (J48)	316	1924
HMS *Oriole* (J110)	441	1910
HMS *Plinlimmon* (J66)	436	1895
HMS *Queen of Thanet* (J30)	792	1916
HMS *Sandown* (J20)	684	1934

THE BRITISH SLOOP HMS *KINGFISHER* AND THE FRENCH NAVAL TRAWLER *LE MOUSSAILLON*

1. HMS *Kingfisher*. The sloop, a name first used during the Age of Sail, referred to a small 'trade protection' vessel, originally designed for service overseas. By 1940, sloops were primarily used as convoy escorts. In the mid-1930s, the Admiralty commissioned the Kingfisher class of coastal sloops (also known as patrol sloops or patrol vessels). These were smaller versions of pre-war sloops, designed as escorts for coastal convoys. HMS *Kingfisher* (L70), namesake of the nine-vessel class, formed part of the 1st Anti-Submarine Flotilla based at Portland, until being sent to join Operation *Dynamo* on 29 May. Most sloops were used to protect the evacuation routes, but *Kingfisher*, under Lt. Cdr. George Harrison, made five runs to Dunkirk, between 31 May and 4 June, and evacuated 638 Allied troops. The ship was damaged, first in an air attack on 1 June, and then, on 4 June, during a collision with a French naval trawler. This shows *Kingfisher*'s appearance during the evacuation. At the time, the sloop's anti-aircraft armament was minimal – just four twin Lewis machine guns.

2. The French naval trawler *Le Moussaillon*. The most numerous type of warship to take part in Operation *Dynamo* was the naval trawler. These had been requisitioned at the start of the war, given a gun or two and commissioned into service with the Royal Navy as either naval trawlers (HMT) or, if smaller drift trawlers, then as naval drifters (HMD). The French Navy did the same, requisitioning trawlers from the coast of the English Channel from Brest to Dunkirk. For the most part, both navies used them as patrol boats, convoy escorts or as minesweepers. Over 120 of these small warships took part in the evacuation, and 18 of them were sunk during the operation. The small French *chalutier à moteur naval* ('naval motor trawler') *Le Moussaillon* (AD79) was typical of these workmanlike vessels. After being requisitioned in Boulogne at the start of the war, the beam trawler was employed as an auxiliary minesweeper in the *Pas de Calais*. In all, under her skipper Lt. P. M. Bourgain, the trawler made two evacuation runs to Dunkirk, rescuing 307 men. *La Moussaillon* was sunk in an air attack on Route X, during the late afternoon of 1 June.

1

2

Vessel	Displacement (tons) – standard	Completed
HMT *Jasper* (T14)	381	1932
HMT *John Cattling* (FY536)	276	1918
HMT *Kingston Alalite* (FY135)	412	1933
HMT *Kingston Andalusite* (FY160)	415	1934
HMT *Kingston Galena* (FY145)	415	1934
HMT *Kingston Olivine* (FY193)	378	1930
HMT *Lady Philomena* (FY148)	417	1936
HMT *Lord Grey* (FY1593)	346	1928
HMT *Lord Inchcape* (FY1611)	338	1924
HMT *Lord Melchett* (FY672)	347	1929
HMT *Olvina* (FY154)	425	1934
HMT *Our Bairns* (FY1566)	275	1917
HMT *Polly Johnson* (H322)*	290	1919
HMT *Saon* (FY159)	386	1933
HMT *Sarah Hide* (FY968)	162	1921
HMT *Sphene* (FY249)	412	1934
HMT *Spurs* (FY168)	399	1933
HMT *St Achilleus* (FY152)*	484	1934
HMT *Stella Dorado* (FY131)*	416	1935
HMT *Strathelliot* (A46)	211	1915
HMT *Thomas Bartlett* (FY553) *	290	1918
HMT *Thrifty* (FY1523)	139	1916
HMT *Viviana* (FY238)	452	1936
HMT *Westella* (FY161)*	413	1934
HMT *Thuringia* (FY106)*	396	1933
HMT *Topaze* (T40)	421	1935
HMT *Velia* (FD49)	290	1914
HMT *Wolves* (FY158)	422	1934

Vessel	Displacement (tons) – standard	Completed
HMS *Snaefell* (J118)	466	1907
HMS *Waverley* (J51)*	537	1899
HMS *Westward Ho* (J43)	460	1894

Paddle anti-aircraft ships (2)

Vessel	Displacement (tons) – standard	Completed
HMS *Crested Eagle**	1,100	1925
HMS *Royal Eagle*	1,539	1932

Naval drifters (16)

Vessel	Displacement (tons) – standard	Completed
HMD *Alcmaria* (FY1525)	148	1916
HMD *Dorienta*	101	1914
HMD *Eileen Emma*	102	1914
HMD *Feasible*	103	1912
HMD *Gervais Rentoul*	100	1917
HMD *Girl Gladys*	111	1917
HMD *Kindred Star*	115	1930
HMD *Lord Collingwood*	116	1930
HMD *Lord Keith*	116	1930
HMD *Lord Rodney*	104	1928
HMD *Lord St Vincent*	115	1929
HMD *Monarda*	108	1916
HMD *Ocean Breeze*	112	1927
HMD *Renascent*	100	1926
HMD *Strive*	102	1912
HMD *Yorkshire Lass*	111	1920

Note: *Drifters under 120 tons weren't allocated a pennant number.*

Armed yachts (9)

Vessel	Displacement (tons) – standard	Completed
HMY *Adventuress*	322	1898
HMY Amulree*	86	1938
HMY *Aronia*	193	1929
HMY *Caleta*	138	1930
HMY *Christabel II*	111	1928
HMY *Grive**	816	1905
HMY *Gulzar*	201	1934
HMY *Sargasso* (FY053)	216	1926
HMY *Taransay* (FY057)	116	1930

* = *Sunk during Operation Dynamo*

Marine Nationale

Destroyers

Bourrasque class | *Bourrasque* (T41), *Cyclone* (T61), *Mistral* (T63), *Siroco* (T62)

Displacement:	1,900 tons (fully laden)	Commissioned:	1926–27
Dimensions:	Length overall: 347' (105.77m), Beam: 31' 9" (9.64m), Draught: 14' 1" (4.3m)		
Propulsion:	Two shafts, two turbines, two boilers	Max speed:	33 knots
Armament:	Four 5.1" (130mm) guns in single mounts, two 37mm AA guns in single mounts, two 0.5" (13.2mm) Hotchkiss AA machine guns in single twin mounting, six 21.65" (45cm) torpedoes in two triple launchers	Complement:	142

Built in 1906, the paddle-wheeler PS *Emperor of India* was a cross-channel mail packet, based for the most part in Bournemouth. The vessel was used as a naval minesweeper during World War I, and was requisitioned again in 1939, serving in the Thames estuary under the command of Lt. Charles Pawley RNR. Here, HMS *Emperor of India* (J106) is pictured returning from Dunkirk with troops, one of three trips made by the auxiliary minesweeper, with a total of 644 Allied troops embarked.

L'Adroit class | *Foudroyant* (T52). Improved Bourrasque class

Displacement:	2,000 tons (fully laden)	Commissioned:	1930
Dimensions:	Length overall: 351′ 8″ (107.2m), Beam: 32′ 3″ (9.84m), Draught: 14′ 1″ (4.3m)		
Propulsion:	Two shafts, two turbines, 3 boilers	Max speed:	33 knots
Armament:	Four 5.1″ (130mm) guns in single mounts, two 37mm AA guns in single mounts, two 13.2mm Hotchkiss AA machine guns in twin mountings, six 21.65″ (45cm) torpedoes in two triple launchers	Complement:	142

Chacal class | *Léopard* (X22)

Displacement:	2,950 tons (fully laden)	Commissioned:	1927
Dimensions:	Length overall: 415′ 11″ (126.78m), Beam: 37′ 2″ (11.32m), Draught: 13′ 5″ (4.1m)		
Propulsion:	Two shafts, two turbines, five boilers	Max speed:	35 knots
Armament:	Four 5.1″ (130mm) guns in single mounts, two 3″ (75mm) AA guns in single mounts, eight 0.5″ (13.2mm) Hotchkiss AA machine guns in four twin mountings, six 21.65″ (45cm) torpedoes in two triple launchers	Complement:	195

Aigle class | *Épervier* (X112)

Displacement:	3,410 tons (fully laden)	Commissioned:	1934
Dimensions:	Length overall: 424′ 2″ (129.3m), Beam: 38′ 10″ (11.84m), Draught: 16′ 4″ (4.97m)		
Propulsion:	Two shafts, two turbines, four boilers	Max speed:	36 knots
Armament:	Five 5.46″ (138.6mm) guns in single mounts, four 3″ (75mm) AA guns in two twin mounts, four 0.5″ (13.2mm) AA machine guns in two twin mountings, seven 21.65″ (45cm) torpedoes in two twin and one triple launcher	Complement:	230

Sloops *(Avisos)*

Arras class | *Arras* (A05), *Belfort* (Q74)

Displacement:	1,370 tons (fully laden)	Commissioned:	1918–20
Dimensions:	Length overall: 246′ 1″ (75m), Beam: 28′ 7″ (8.7m), Draught: 10′ 6″ (3.2m)		
Propulsion:	Two shafts, two turbines, two boilers	Max speed:	20 knots
Armament:	Two 5.1″ (130mm) guns in single mounts, one 3″ (75mm) gun in single mount, four 0.5″ (13.2mm) Hotchkiss AA machine guns in single mountings	Complement:	104

Bougainville class | *Savorgnan de Brazza* (A03) | Colonial service sloop

Displacement:	2,600 tons (fully laden)	Commissioned:	1932
Dimensions:	Length overall: 340′ 3″ (103.7m), Beam: 41′ 8″ (12.7m), Draught: 14′ 9″ (4.5m)		
Propulsion:	Two shafts, two diesel engines	Max speed:	18 knots
Armament:	Three 5.46″ (138.6mm) guns in single mounts, four 37mm AA guns in single mounts, six 0.5″ (13.2mm) Hotchkiss AA machine guns in three twin mountings. Designed to carry a float plane, but aircraft was not installed in 1940.	Complement:	183

Minesweepers

Élan class | *Commandant Delage* (A12), *Commandant Riviere* (A32), *L'Impétueuse* (A35), *La Bodeuse* (A18)

Displacement:	895 tons (fully laden)	Commissioned	1939–40
Dimensions:	Length overall: 256' 11" (78.3m), Beam: 28 6" (8.7m), Draught: 10' 9" (3.28m)		
Propulsion:	Two shafts, two diesel engines	Max speed:	20 knots
Armament:	Two 3.9" (100mm) guns in single mounts, eight 0.5" (13.2mm) Hotchkiss AA machine guns in four twin mountings	Complement:	106

Torpedo-Boats

La Melpomène class | *Bouclier* (T141), *Branlebas* (T113), *La Flore* (T143), *L'Incomprise* (T112)

Displacement:	895 tons (fully laden)	Commissioned:	1937–38
Dimensions:	Length overall: 264' 9" (80.7m), Beam: 26' 1" (7.96m), Draught: 10' 1" (3.07m)		
Propulsion:	Two shafts, two turbines, two boilers	Max speed:	34½ knots
Armament:	Two 3.9" (100mm) guns in single mounts, four 0.5" (13.2mm) Hotchkiss AA machine guns in two twin mountings, two 21.65" (45cm) torpedoes in twin launcher	Complement:	105

Gunboat

Friponne class | *Diligente* | Colonial service gunboat

Displacement:	455 tons (fully laden)	Commissioned:	1916
Dimensions:	Length overall: 217' 10" (66.4m), Beam: 23' (7m), Draught: 8' 10" (2.8m)		
Propulsion:	Two shafts, two diesel engines	Max speed:	14½ knots
Armament:	Two 3.9" (100mm) guns in single mounts, two 0.5" (13.2mm) Hotchkiss AA machine guns in single mountings	Complement:	54

Smaller auxiliary vessels

Armed trawlers

Vessel	Displacement (tons) – standard	Completed	Vessel	Displacement (tons) – standard	Completed
André Louis (AD27)	284	1907	*Jean Bart* (VP2)	-	-
Angèle Marie (AD71)	238	1929	*La Nantaise* (P135)	403	1933
Bernadette (AD90)	302	1914	*Le Chasse Marée* (AD94)	251	1920
Cap d'Antifer (AD69)	294	1912	*Le Moussaillon* (AD79)	183	1923
Denis Papan (AD48)*	309	1917	*Louise et Marie* (AD2)	265	1916
Dijonnais (AD33)	389	1934	*Marguerite Rose* (AD23)*	409	1931
Edmond-René (AD51)	288	1907	*Monique-Camille* (AD25)	277	1934
Emile Deschamps (AD20)*	349	1922	*Patrie* (P36)	754	1920
Emma (AD89)*	255	1902	*Président Briand* (AD108)	227	1932
Gaston Rivier (AD21)	315	1918	*Reine des Flots* (P39)	608	1923
Gâtinais (AD43)	389	1933	*Vénus* (AD74)	264	1906
Henri Louis (AD397)	-	-			

Naval drifters

Vessel	Displacement (tons) – standard	Completed	Vessel	Displacement (tons) – standard	Completed
Caporal Peugeot (AD9)	102	1923	*Lucien Gougy* (AD28)	150	1935
Jean Ribault (AD81)	153	1933	*Maria Eléna* (AD54)	146	1932

Naval patrol ships (former cargo vessels)

Cérons (P21) and *Sauternes* (P22) were French cargo ships, taken into service in late 1939 and converted into auxiliary patrol vessels. They were both built in the same yard at La Trait on the River Seine, and made their maiden voyages in 1922–23. Each displaced 1,049 tons (standard), and was powered by a single screw and engine, giving them a maximum speed of 10 to 10½ knots. After their conversion, they were both armed with four 3.9" (100mm) guns in single mounts and a single 37mm AA gun.

Civilian vessels

In addition, numerous French civilian ships were used in the evacuation, including 15 cargo ships, four passenger ships and two tankers. Of these, two of the cargo ships, one of the passenger ships and both tankers were sunk by German aircraft. The French also used a makeshift flotilla of 19 smaller vessels: 14 trawlers, four tugs and a dredger. Two of these, a tug and the dredger, were lost.

FURTHER READING

Atkin, Ronald, *Pillar of Fire: Dunkirk 1940*, Sidgwick & Jackson Ltd, London (1990)

Brann, Christian, *Little Ships of Dunkirk*, Collectors' Books Ltd, Cirencester (1989)

Campbell, John, *Naval Weapons of World War Two*, Conway Maritime Press, London (1982)

Friedman, Norman, *British Destroyers: The Second World War and After*, Seaforth Publishing, Barnsley (2008)

Friedman, Norman, *British Destroyers: From the Earliest Days to the Second World War*, Seaforth Publishing, Barnsley (2009)

Gardiner, Robert, *Conway's All the World's Fighting Ships 1922–1946*, Conway Maritime Press, London (1980)

Gardner, W.J.R. (ed.), *The Evacuation from Dunkirk: 'Operation Dynamo', 26 March – 4 June 1940*, Routledge (Naval Staff Histories series), Abingdon (2000)

Hawkins, Ian (ed.), *Destroyer: An Anthology of First-Hand Accounts of the War at Sea, 1939–45*, Conway Maritime Press, London (2003)

Jackson, Robert, *Dunkirk: The British Evacuation, 1940*, Weidenfeld & Nicolson, London (2012)

Lavery, Brian, *Churchill's Navy: The Ships, Men and Organisation, 1939–45*, Conway Maritime Press, London (2006)

Lord, Walter, *The Miracle of Dunkirk: The True Story of Operation Dynamo*, Viking Press, New York, NY (1983)

Lund, Paul & Ludnam, Harry, *Trawlers Go to War: The Story of Harry Tate's Navy*, W. Foulsham & Co., Slough (1971)

Mace, Martin, *The Royal Navy at Dunkirk: Commanding Officers' Accounts of British Warships in Action during Operation Dynamo*, Frontline Books, London (2017)

Pearce, M.J. & Burnell-Nugent, Sir James; *Dunkirk – Operation Dynamo 26th May – 4th June 1940: An Epic of Gallantry*, Paul Honeywill [Britannia Royal Naval Histories of World War II], Dartmouth (2021)

Preston, Antony, *V and W Class Destroyers, 1917–45*, Macdonald & Co., London (1971)

Roskill, S.W., *The War at Sea Vol. 1 'The Defensive'*, HMSO, London (1954)

Scott, Peter, *The Battle of the Narrow Seas*, Country Life Ltd, London (1945)

Thompson, Peter, *Dunkirk: Retreat to Victory*, Arcade Publishing, New York, NY (2011)

Weir, Philip, *Dunkirk and the Little Ships*, Shire Publications, Oxford (2020)

Winser, John de S., *BEF Ships before, at and after Dunkirk*, World Ship Society, London (1999)

INDEX